COPING WITH AIDS

COPING WITH

AIDS

Facts

& Fears

Morton L. Kurland, M.D.

(1988 Edition: Completely Revised and Updated)

THE ROSEN PUBLISHING GROUP, INC.
NEW YORK

Published in 1988 by The Rosen Publishing Group, Inc.
29 East 21st Street, New York, NY 10010

First Edition

Library of Congress Cataloging-in-Publication Data

Kurland, Morton L.
   Coping with AIDS.

   Includes bibliographies and index.
   1. AIDS (Disease)—Popular works.   I. Title.
[DNLM: 1. Acquired Immunodeficiency Syndrome—
popular works.   WD 308 K96c]
RC607.A26K87   1986   616.97′92   86–15471
ISBN 0–8239–0779–1

Manufactured in the United States of America

Acknowledgments

In the course of preparing this book the author has taken advantage of many sources, including the published materials listed in the Bibliography. A good many of these books have been invaluable in understanding the workings of the immune system, the white blood cells, antibodies, and the depredations of the acquired immune deficiency syndrome virus in attacking the system.

The author wishes to express his thanks specifically to the staff of the Del Webb Memorial Library at the Eisenhower Medical Center.

In addition, the invaluable assistance of the medical and nursing staffs at Eisenhower Memorial Hospital in gathering material relating to patients, their diseases, their families, and the problems of the staff itself is acknowledged. The specific assistance of two physicians, Lawrence Cone, M.D., and Milan Fiala, M.D., should be mentioned as sources of information about AIDS and of scientific data obtainable only from journals and current meetings. Both doctors are experts in the field of virology and infectious diseases and have been conducting extensive research in the treatment and, it is hoped, cure of acquired immune deficiency syndrome.

The author also wishes to acknowledge the following publications as sources for many of the graphs, charts and statistics relating to the disease.

USPHS *Centers for Disease Control Weekly Report*
American Medical News, a publication of the American
Medical Association
California Physician, a publication of the California
Medical Association
The Western Journal of Medicine
The New England Journal of Medicine
The Journal of the American Medical Association

As always, the author wishes to acknowledge the invaluable assistance, hard work, and know-how of Ruth Scott, who has helped to prepare this manuscript word by word.

Finally, in addition to the usual proofreading, corrections, and eagle-eyed assistance that she has always provided, the author wishes to express gratitude to Adrienne M. Kurland, R.N., for the medical illustrations included in the book.

Contents

Introduction

The disease known as acquired immune deficiency syndrome was first described several years ago. It was then thought to be confined to an exotic portion of the population of this country and, indeed, of the world. The victims initially seemed to be confined to Haitians and the homosexual population. After a time it became evident that people who used intravenous drugs were also affected. A suspicion began to grow that the disease was caused by a virus. It seemed to be related either to blood transmission or, in some way, sexual activity. The first thought was that gays who engaged in anal sexual practices were the primary victims. Researchers postulated that the bacteria and fungi that live in the rectal and anal areas were related to the disease. Repeated anal intercourse was believed to be its cause. Why Haitians also contracted it was not clear.

Some people and, in fact, a number of evangelical religious leaders postulated that AIDS was divine punishment for the sins of the victims. An almost smug attitude developed among the general population that this was the kind of disease that its victims probably deserved. Nevertheless, as the disease became more widespread and its depredations became evident throughout the western world, general concern increased. Many prominent persons were diagnosed as having the disease or were dying from it. Film stars and television personalities were named. Still, these celebrities were either known or suspected homosexuals or accidental victims through blood transfusions. As the fear of blood transmission became more widespread, the general population became increasingly worried. The term AIDS became known all over the United States. Discussions were held about ways to protect the blood transfusion and replacement system against the virus.

Money was appropriated for further research. Concern was voiced about people being accidentally infected in hospitals or even coming in contact with the virus in public places such as restaurants, rest rooms, and theaters.

It still seemed, however, that most people were "not involved." There was an eerie similarity to those in allied countries during World War II who heard rumors about Hitler's holocaust but preferred not to believe them. Even then, some self-righteously decided that the victims probably deserved it and chose to do nothing about it. Not many paid attention to the warning given us by the poet John Donne, who wrote that "no man is an island, entire of itself." Most people's familiarity with Donne's work was the single line, ". . . never send to know for whom the bell tolls; it tolls for thee." *For Whom the Bell Tolls* is remembered as the title of a book about the Spanish Civil War by Ernest Hemingway. The rest, including the message, is forgotten. Donne's point was that something that affects any portion of humanity does in fact affect all of us.

The poet's warning has now come painfully true for all of us. The AIDS virus is no longer an affliction limited to those considered by some as the outcasts of society. It is more than something that bothers a small ethnic group in the Caribbean or a group of people with different sexual preferences than most of us, or even the tragic victims of drug addiction. It now promises to be widespread throughout the entire heterosexual society. The AIDS virus knows no ethnic boundaries, no sexual preference, and no diagnostic category. It can affect anyone and now appears to be doing so.

Casual sexual contact, part of the "sexual revolution" of the 60's, 70's, and 80's, has now become a potentially lethal undertaking. Having sex with someone you don't know can mean acquiring a disease that can kill you. Since the signs of the disease don't appear until several years after the infection is contracted, anyone is a potential carrier. Anyone whom you don't know is potentially infected.

It is no longer possible to be smug, self-righteous, or safe behind our oceans of propriety. The "straight" population of our society is at risk. A holocaust far surpassing anything the Nazis imagined can engulf the world. One might even say that the survival of our species is at risk.

Years ago the poet T.S. Eliot predicted that when the world ends it will do so "not with a bang but a whimper." Instead of a sudden fiery nuclear blast, our society may well be wiped out silently and slowly by an infectious agent. The killer of mankind, unlike the mushroom cloud that has haunted the nightmares of millions for years, could well be a semiliving bit of protein so small that it cannot be seen even with a high-powered microscope.

AIDS is known to be caused by a submicroscopic virus, an infectious particle so small that it can be seen only by the reflected light of an electron microscope. Although not living itself, the virus enters living cells and becomes part of them. It becomes alive by joining living tissue: ours, yours, and mine. Any virus has that capability. Examples are the common cold, herpes, hepatitis, and several varieties of influenza.

Those of us who have worked in hospitals and outpatient clinics where victims of AIDS are treated recognize the enormity of the problem. Young men with sallow complexions, thin to the point of emaciation, walk slowly through the halls as if in a dream, their skin mottled with the huge purplish and black discoloration characteristic of a skin tumor (Kaposi's sarcoma) that was almost unheard of before the advent of AIDS. These young people (now mostly men) have an almost haunted look of despair. They appear to have given up hope entirely and to be simply waiting for their lives to come to an end. Their world is ending with the quietest of whimpers.

Now that AIDS is beginning to spread to the heterosexual population, the disease threatens the very fabric of society itself. Like the Black Plague of the Middle Ages, which destroyed almost the entire population of Europe, an AIDS epidemic could ruin the civilized world. By attacking and killing the individuals biologically most suited for reproduction, it strikes at the heart of the survival of our species. It can even pass across the placental barrier into the blood of an unborn fetus. Beyond saving the whales, we now have to deal seriously with saving the humans.

A major purpose of this book is to provide another point of view not only for the victims but for you adolescents, your loved ones, your families and friends. We shall describe what the disease is and how it can be prevented, controlled, and ultimately cured.

The universe is said to have started with a "big bang." The end of humanity in the universe does not have to be with the whimper of an insidious disease. There are means to fight the threat of AIDS. Let us see how we can proceed to do so.

CHAPTER 1

What Is AIDS?

The term AIDS has become a frightening label in our times. Headlines shout it forth in huge letters. Television stories use the word with frightening implications that it stands for terror and anxiety. What is it really?

Simply put, AIDS is an acronym; that is, a shorthand way of saying something. AIDS stands for acquired immune deficiency syndrome.

Syndrome, of course, is simply a term for a set of symptoms that are found in a particular illness. All illnesses have syndromes. Colds show themselves when people get a fever, a cough, a running nose, and a general feeling of being ill. That is a syndrome.

Immune deficiency means that the systems in our bodies that protect us from diseases are deficient, or not working well. The immune system is that part of our body that renders us immune to outside invaders, that is, germs and small single-celled organisms that try to live within us as unwanted guests. Under normal circumstances our immune system attacks and destroys them. That is why human beings have been able to survive for millions of years in a complex world. The immune system protects us from bacterial attack. When it is deficient, it allows our bodies to be open to invading foreign substances.

Something acquired is simply something that is derived from the outside as compared to something with which we are born. In some cases infants are born without an adequate immune system. We have seen pictures on television of children living in plastic bubbles, protective tents that keep out germs and the kinds of alien substances that can cause illness. When this lack of immunity happens because it is acquired, it is given the name AIDS.

In summary then, AIDS is a disease that is acquired from outside and is caused by a germ. In this case, the germ is a virus.

What Is a Virus?

A virus is a tiny particle of protein which when it is joined to living matter becomes alive itself. The virus does not live unless it is actually within a host organism. The host organisms can be animals, birds, or even reptiles. In this instance the host organisms are people. The virus lives only inside of us. When it is outside, it is simply a piece of protein awaiting life by entering a living creature.

A virus is so small that it cannot be seen even under an ordinary microscope that can be used to see certain colonies of germs. To see a virus we must look at it in reflected light on a viewing screen called an electron microscope. The electron microscope, an invention of modern technology, throws particles of electrons onto substances that are too small to be seen by lenses. The shadows of these particles are then visible, much as a television picture can show us images from thousands of miles away by illuminating sensitive plates on a video tube. The electron microscope has allowed us to examine viruses and to understand more about them.

Because they are so small and are found everywhere, it is difficult to deal with viruses until they start to cause damage. The virus responsible for AIDS had been identified and named. Originally it was called HTLV III. Recently the name has been changed to HIV 1 and HIV 2 to help us understand its various changes and disguises.

As we have seen, a virus is a substance that lives inside body cells and in its activity destroys those cells. The AIDS virus destroys the cells that act as the policemen of the body with the job of attacking, destroying, and cleaning up invading substances.

It may be helpful to compare viruses to other organisms in size. Viruses are much smaller than the bacteria that cause such diseases as strep throat, most kinds of pneumonia, and the skin infections called pimples or, when they are worse, carbuncles. Bacteria can be seen under the microscope and can be treated with a number of substances called antibiotics. Penicillin was the first antibiotic to be widely known; today hundreds do the same job.

Other organisms called fungi are extremely tiny plantlike creatures that can grow inside the body, on the surface of the skin, in the mouth, or elsewhere and multiply to cause painful and dangerous infections. Fungi can be seen with a microscope, and when a fungus spreads widely it can be seen with the naked eye. Most fungus infections are found in tropical climates because the warm and damp environment is conducive to their growth.

There are even small animals called amoebae and paramecia that can cause diseases. They are responsible for dysentery and other disorders of the digestive tract that people contract when they travel to foreign countries. These, too, can be seen by microscope, and agents are available to attack and destroy them.

Only the virus has so far eluded our efforts to kill it inside the body. Our major protection against viruses has to be prevention. Over the years we have learned something about viral infections, since they have been with us as long as we have existed on the planet.

CAN WE FIGHT VIRUSES?

In years gone by man recognized that illnesses were attacking him but was unable to find a way to cure them. At the beginning of scientific investigation a disease called smallpox was the first one to be conquered.

Smallpox is a highly contagious disease that causes high fever and multiple skin eruptions. It still exists in certain parts of the world and is extremely deadly. The virus that causes smallpox can be transmitted through the air, so that people coughing or sneezing can spread it to other people. Two or three weeks after the initial exposure, the new victim becomes feverish and has aches and pains all over the body. He finally is unable to stand or walk and may finally die as the virus spreads throughout the body.

Jenner

Attempts continued for centuries to cope with smallpox. It was not until Edward Jenner (1749–1823), an English physician, began experimenting with a disease called cowpox that a treatment was found. Jenner discovered that people who worked in dairies seemed to be immune to smallpox plagues. He deduced that was because they had been exposed earlier to cowpox, a much less deadly disease that could be overcome by the body's defenses. After the exposure to cowpox had occurred, the same system of defense, that is, the immune system, was sufficient to kill the smallpox virus as well.

Jenner then did something that has marked human progress over the centuries and made it so remarkable: He had an idea.

Jenner's idea was that if everyone were exposed to cowpox, wouldn't it be likely that they, too, would become immune to smallpox? He decided to experiment. Finding some people with cowpox, he scraped pus from the eruptions on their skin and scratched it into the skin of otherwise healthy people. Sure enough, they developed cowpox too. After they had overcome the cowpox, they were in time immune to smallpox as well.

Eventually Jenner called his system vaccination. He had discovered that by enlisting the assistance of the body's own immune system to overcome a less dangerous virus in the body, he could help to conquer a deadly disease.

Jenner lived long before the Nobel prizes, but he certainly deserved one. The same principle is now used to protect children against poliomyelitis or infantile paralysis. The discoverer of the vaccine, Jonas E. Salk, did win a Congressional Gold Medal.

Researchers are still working on ways of vaccinating people against AIDS and other viral diseases such as influenza and hepatitis.

Koch

Other men have had ideas too, ideas that have been markers for human progress in mankind's ancient struggle for survival.

Robert Koch (1843–1910) was a German bacteriologist

who did most of his work in the late 1800's. A country doctor in Prussia, he spent much time studying bacteria under the newly perfected microscope. Dr. Koch established the fact that bacteria cause many infectious diseases and even identified the ones that cause such terrible diseases as tuberculosis, anthrax, wound infections, and cholera.

It was Koch who first described "the scientific method," the specific form of research in which one starts with a theory of how a disease is spread, follows that theory from beginning to end, and then tries to reproduce it on another occasion to prove that it is correct.

Toward the end of his life Robert Koch received the 1905 Nobel prize in medicine and physiology for his work on such diseases as sleeping sickness, malaria, tuberculosis, and bubonic plague.

Pasteur

Men and women from all over the world have contributed to our ongoing struggle against illness. A French scientist, not a physician but a chemist, began studying bacteria in the 1800's. He was Louis Pasteur (1822–1895), and he perfected the technique of vaccination against anthrax and rabies. He also lent his name to the process that protects milk against germs. The process, pasteurization, is also used to protect wine and beer from being damaged by undesirable organisms.

The Pasteur Institute in Paris is a major center of learning and research. Many studies are currently under way at the Institute in efforts to deal with the AIDS virus.

Ehrlich

While scientists such as Jenner, Pasteur, and Koch were seeking to understand more about the enemies that attack us, another German, Paul Ehrlich, was trying to find a specific cure for diseases. He was looking for what he called "the magic bullet."

Ehrlich believed that if he could find the right chemical it would, like a bullet, pierce a microscopic enemy and kill it. He engaged in hundreds of experiments with various chemicals in an attempt to kill the germ that causes syphilis.

Syphilis is caused by a tiny organism similar to the amoeba and the paramecium. Called a spirochete, it is a single-celled organism that invades the blood cells, destroying them and causing a disease that ultimately kills the victim. Erhlich tested innumerable chemicals to no avail. Eventually, the six hundred sixth experiment yielded an agent that was useful in destroying the syphilis germ. He first called it 606 and later Salvarsan. It was used successfully in the treatment of syphilis until penicillin came along, almost fifty years later.

We are still looking for magic bullets to shoot at the AIDS virus. It is hoped that the Erhlichs, the Jenners, the Kochs and Pasteurs in Germany, France, England, America, the Soviet Union, and everywhere else that men labor in laboratories will come up with an answer to today's challenge.

Fleming

Sir Alexander Fleming (1881–1955) was an Englishman who had another idea. He was working in his laboratory at the beginning of World War II, growing some bacteria on culture plates. One of his culture plates was left open and became contaminated by a fungus that was in the air.

Fleming, unlike thousands of others who preceded him and who threw away the fungus growing on the plate, instead looked at the plate and thought about it.

The area around the fungus was free of bacteria. The bacteria grew everywhere else, but where the fungus had landed the bacteria had died. Probably thousands of people had seen this phenomenon and thought nothing of it. Fleming did something they hadn't done. He thought and he had an idea.

Fleming's idea was that something in the fungus had killed the germs. If he could extract that material from the fungus, perhaps he could kill the germs, too. That substance he later called penicillin. It was the beginning of the antibiotic era in medicine. It was saved millions of lives and truly changed the face of the world, and it all came about because of a thought, an idea, and a lot of hard work.

Today's Challenge

Today we are faced with the challenge of still another deadly disease, the latest and potentially the most lethal of all. It attacks people who are in the reproductive phase of life, people who should be responsible for future generations. By destroying these people the disease can threaten the existence of the human race.

The disease attacks venereally; that is, through sexual activity, and through a few other channels. It is the responsibility of everyone to understand the disease and how it is transmitted and to deal with it head-on.

CHAPTER 2

Safe Sex?

To speak of "safe sex" in this day and age is not as silly as it might have sounded only ten years ago. Sex can be dangerous because it can lead to the transmission of a life-threatening disease. Even in generations gone by there was danger of contracting diseases through sexual activity, and for a period of time they were life-threatening as well.

We have seen how Paul Ehrlich was able to discover "a magic bullet" to attack the spirochete that causes syphilis. The magic bullet did succeed in killing the invader, and later penicillin was even more effective. Before their discovery, however, safe sex was an issue discussed as seriously in the 1800's and earlier as AIDS is today. Syphilis was potentially a killer. It destroyed people years after it was acquired just as AIDS does now, and it was contracted during sexual activity when people were at their most vulnerable. It's hard to think about catching a disease or being vulnerable to infection when you are in the heat of passion. When your feelings are aroused and your only interest is in getting close to another human being for sexual activity, it becomes easy to blot out all the problems that this might bring with it. For that reason we have to think about the problems *in advance* and prepare ourselves accordingly.

Since AIDS is primarily a disease of sexual transmission, that is where our focus has to lie. In later chapters we shall discuss the transmission of AIDS through blood contacts such as infected needles, scratches on the skin, and the like.

Not for Me?

At the beginning of the AIDS epidemic it seemed that the only people at risk were homosexual persons who engaged in anal intercourse, and it was easy for people who were not in that category to say, "Not me, I'm safe, I don't have to worry about those people."

All of these safe positions have now capitulated to the onslaught of the invader. There is no safety, and there is no foxhole for the heterosexual in today's society. All of us are at risk as long as we engage in sexual activity with a partner whom we do not know and whose blood has not been tested or whose blood tests have not been confirmed as safe.

What does safe mean? If a person's blood test is nonreactive to the HIV 1 virus, it means that the person has not been exposed to the virus within the past thirty to ninety days. It takes that long for the body to react to the presence of a foreign body in some cases. The body reacts to being challenged by a foreign protein by developing an antitoxin reaction, but that reaction takes time to occur. A blood test made today and reported as nonreactive would be taken to mean that the person tested has not been exposed to the AIDS virus and is free of infection. The catch, however, is that because it takes thirty to ninety days for a person to develop a reaction to the virus, he or she could have been exposed one, two, or three months before and still not have developed the immune response.

Logically, that means that a person is not safe until he or she is still nonreactive after ninety days.

How Safe Is Safe?

To be totally safe we would have to assume that a person had a blood test that was reported normal and then had no sexual contacts for a minimum of ninety days. After that time, the blood test should be repeated. If it is still normal, it is probable that sex can be carried on without infecting a partner.

Even that is not foolproof, however, as all tests have false positives and negatives. The only totally safe sex is no sex at all. Considering human nature, it is unreasonable to ask people never to have sex. Besides, it would end human life if they obeyed. Given the general understanding that sex is reasonably safe after the blood test remains negative for ninety days, we are within some boundaries of safety.

Even so, there is still another precaution that both sexes need to use regularly. The only safety that one can have against a virus invading an area where the protective armor of the body is broken by a cut, a sore, or even an abrasion, is by having an extra layer of protection. In this instance, the condom seems an answer.

What Is a Condom?

A condom is a protective sheath that a man can place over his penis to prevent the spread of germs. Initially, it was intended to prevent the spread of gonorrhea or syphilis; coincidentally it came to be used as a method of contraception. We all know that the use of "rubbers" keeps the semen from entering the vagina and therefore prevents conception—unless the condom ruptures.

Even more important at this time is that the condom represents an added shield to protect both partners. The man who uses a condom is protected against any germ or virus that may be present in the female organs, and the woman is protected against the AIDS virus, which is highly concentrated in the sperm of the male.

Use of the condom is actually far more important for a woman than for a man. The reasons have to do with anatomy.

The woman, in effect, is the receptacle for the male sperm. Her organs are passive in nature and remain in place when the male organ enters and leaves her body. The sperm are deposited inside her body in the vaginal vault, the area around the cervix at the end of the uterus where the sperm enter. If there is even a slight abrasion or sore on the cervix or in any part of the vagina and the semen contains virus, there is an opening for the virus to enter the body. Since we know that AIDS enters through the blood, any small area of bleeding or irritation can be the portal for the invasion of this deadly enemy.

The fact is that semen, when it enters the female body, can remain in the vaginal area for several days unless the woman carefully cleans her vagina by douching (and even that is not certain). That is not the case with the man, of course. He can enter the female anatomy sexually and then remove his sexual organ, with much less opportunity for exposure to the virus. This is because of the short time spent in contact with the female genitalia and because exposure to air and the environment in general kills the virus.

The virus is much safer inside the vagina and can remain infectious after the sperm itself has died.

Many women have erosions and other small sores on the cervix. By itself this is not dangerous, but exposing even a small sore to the AIDS virus is extremely dangerous.

It now should be obvious why the use of condoms is vital. It has nothing to do with contraception, although contraception may be achieved. Other methods of contraception such as a diaphragm or vaginal foam probably do not help at all to defend against the AIDS virus. The condom is a shield behind which the woman is protected, a shield against the semen entering and remaining in her body.

Your Best Protection

It becomes imperative for the female to insist that her partner use a condom in every kind of sexual activity unless they are specifically interested in reproducing.

It is the custom of the author to advise use of condoms by all the young people who seek advice concerning venereal diseases, AIDS, and their general concern about "safe sex." Some young people are not even familiar with the concept. Condoms are obtainable in every pharmacy, and in recent months they have even been advertised on television. Although they are not foolproof, they represent our current best protection against any bacteria or viruses that are transmitted in cells or body fluids. Since the virus lives inside of various cells, the condom is a barrier to those cells and therefore an effective protection against the spread of disease.

Condoms are inexpensive, easily obtained, and disposable. Young people used to be embarrassed to go into a pharmacy and ask for a package of condoms. These days it is an intelligent choice and should be done as a matter of course. Young women are encouraged to purchase condoms personally if they have any expectation of having sexual activity or are not sure that their partner will have them available. Since women are far more at risk than men, they are the ones who need to be more concerned. The protection of the condom is far more important than the momentary embarrassment of going into a pharmacy and buying a package of them.

Some young men object to the use of condoms, saying that it decreases their sexual gratification because of the artificial barrier of latex between their skin and that of their partner. This is a small price to pay for protection on both sides. Anyone who is concerned about his health and welfare, as well as that of his partner, will understand that and agree. Anyone who does not agree is probably so self-centered that he is not the kind of person one would want as an intimate partner. An intimate partner should be a person who cares about you very strongly and who wants your welfare. To tolerate a small inconvenience in order to protect another person is a tiny sacrifice. Those who do not want to make this sacrifice should probably be avoided.

I have advised young women who have consulted me to insist on the use of condoms by their partner, and if the partner refuses, to avoid intimate contact with him. This is the only way to serve their best interests, and if the other person doesn't understand, it is probably best not to deal with him any further.

The same advice is valid for young men. Although less crucial to their health, it is important for them to understand that use of condoms is in the best interest of their partner and does have some value for them as well.

Openness Is Vital

The next problem is how to bring up with a potential partner the use of the condom and even the question of the absence or presence of a positive blood test.

It is essential to have a history of your potential partner's sexual activity. It seems reasonable to assume that a person who has never engaged in sexuality will be free of sexual disease. With the exception of someone who has contracted the disease by accident through a surgical procedure or blood transfusion, or through being a doctor, nurse, or dentist, there will be no risk of venereal disease.

One really must get to know one's sexual partner. This has always been true, but in recent decades it seems to have been lost in the shuffle. Casual intimacy in high school and college has become commonplace. The "sexual revolution" has dictated that people not pry into the intimate background of other people nor be concerned about their multiple sexual experiences. In theory this protects our privacy and individuality. In practice it is no longer reasonable.

You have to have some idea about your potential sexual partner's history. If the partner has a background of wide exposure with a variety of people, he or she represents a significant danger.

The best way to learn about someone's background is in conversation and gaining a general understanding of each other's life history. The longer you know someone and the more comfortable you feel in talking, the more you can find out about that history.

These days it is imperative to get to know the other person as deeply as you can. Sex on the first date is obviously fraught with danger. There is no way to tell by looking at a person whether he or she has had a wide variety of sexual encounters or none at all. There are no telltale signs of AIDS until it is far too late to do anything about it. A person can carry the AIDS virus for three, four, or five years before having any symptoms of the disease at all.

You have to talk with someone at length to find out if he or she has had a wide degree of exposure. If it appears that there is no likelihood of intimacy between you, you can forget the subject altogether and talk about movies, television, good books, and your next political science exam. If you expect things to go further, the conversation must become deeper and an understanding must be reached.

The Risk Is Great

The level of the understanding has to do with an agreement on both sides. Both partners must understand that they are at risk with someone with whom they have never had sex. The risk is real and even potentially fatal. When your life is at stake you have to take time and energy to do research into the danger.

It is not a small thing to risk your life, nor is it a major effort to ask about another person's sexual activity. The better you know the person, the easier it is to ask. Therefore, several dates probably would serve to get answers most comfortably. After knowing someone for a while, you can begin to ask whether or not he or she has had wide experience. If the answer is yes, it might be reasonable to say something like, "Haven't you been afraid of contracting AIDS?"

You can then proceed from a general feeling about AIDS to more specific questions. It wouldn't be unreasonable to say, "If you've had a few sexual encounters with people that you haven't known very well, have you ever considered getting an AIDS test?"

The other person could easily say that he or she had had a blood test and that it was normal. Of course, there is no way to know whether it is true.

Another response might be: "I've thought a lot about this, and I've decided that I'm not going to have sex in the future unless both parties have a negative blood test."

Depending upon the attitude of the other person, the conversation could go further or not. If the other person does not want to have anything to do with blood tests or does not believe they are of any value, I would advise politely but definitely removing yourself from the relationship. Anyone whose mind is so closed as not to be interested in even considering a blood test or giving you the reassurance of such a test is not likely to be a responsible sexual partner anyway.

If you become convinced that the other person has never had any sexual exposure and has never had a blood transfusion or worked in an area where AIDS was present, sex might be permissible—assuming, of cource, that you yourself had never been exposed. Even if this were the case, however, it might be reassuring to the other person for both of you to have a blood test.

You should always keep in mind that it takes thirty to ninety days and possibly longer for a reaction to occur from exposure to the AIDS virus. If you have decided to have intimate relations with someone who had a negative blood test or no exposure to sex, you would also have to be convinced that he or she would not later or at the same time engage in sexual activities outside of your relations. The person could be exposed separately by having sex with a third party and not be aware of it. This can occur even after a negative blood test has been obtained. During the ninety-day waiting period that I advocate, you have to be pretty sure that your potential partner is a serious person and just as worried as you are about contracting AIDS.

How to Begin the Discussion

Here are some ideas for starting a conversation with a new friend so that you can begin talking about this delicate issue. If you yourself are shy or if the person that you need to talk with is shy, too, these may help:

"Did you see the story in last week's newspaper about the AIDS epidemic?"

There doesn't have to be a particular story in last week's newspaper. There are always stories about AIDS in the papers; they can be found almost every day of the week. The important thing is to bring up the subject so that the other person can be open to talking about it.

If the first question doesn't get the two of you into a discussion about the disease, how it is communicated, and the problems in heterosexual sex, you may have to give some stronger hints and talk more yourself. For instance:

"Some people say that AIDS can destroy the whole world. They say it could be just like the bubonic plague in the Middle Ages."

This may give your shy or reluctant other person a chance to talk about the disease and how it is carried. Then you can get into the fact that it is a venereal disease and is spread sexually.

If those openers don't work, there are still other ways to get into the talk. For instance, you can say:

"Did you see the Rock Hudson movie on TV the other night? Rock Hudson really looked good in that movie, not the way we saw him in the newspapers before he died."

This can give you a chance to talk about how a famous person contracted the disease and the disastrous effect it had on him. The other person may then respond and open up the discussion.

If that doesn't work, there are other similar openings. For instance, you can say:

"I saw a commercial for Liberace records on TV last night. What do you think about him?"

Again, it gives you a chance to let the other person talk about AIDS first, and it might open up the discussion more easily than directly entering into it.

If the other person still doesn't pick up the cue, you will have to give stronger hints and be more specific if you are going to get into it at all. By this time, it might seem that the other person is reluctant to discuss the matter. That itself might be important for you to know.

You could say, for instance:

"They say that having sex without using a condom is like going out in a blizzard without an overcoat. The exposure can kill you."

That is a lot stronger. By this time if your friend hasn't picked up the cue, there is a good possibility that he or she doesn't want to talk about it at all. One way to handle this is to follow up with:

"What do you think?"

If that doesn't work, you are probably not going to be able to talk about the issue at all. If you cannot make any meaningful contact, you will have to consider another partner.

The Next Step

If your friend does begin to talk about AIDS and how serious it can be, and even talk about condoms and the protection that they can afford, you can go further into the discussion. It is very important to make your position crystal clear.

An easy way to talk about things that are important to you and that you want to drive home strongly is to *quote authorities*. That is, you can talk about facts that you have read, either in a newspaper or in this book. It is always useful to quote some authority, and since you are reading this book now, you can use it as your source. You can even offer to lend the book to your friend so that he or she can understand what you're talking about.

There are a number of television programs and stories about AIDS and even some commercials for condoms. All of these can be used as points of departure to talk about your feelings, your ideas.

The most important thing that you then must convey is your feeling about blood tests. This is your most important measure in dealing with AIDS. You must make it abundantly clear that you take it seriously and that it is something that must be done if any personal relationship is to go forward.

The Time Factor

When you finally get to the point of talking about the specifics of blood tests for both parties, it is extremely important to understand the time factor.

AIDS is a virus that invades the body, and it takes the body some time to react to it. While the body is developing a reaction to an invading virus, the virus is still present and the host is infectious to other people.

That means that it takes the body thirty, sixty, or even ninety days before a blood reaction is evident. Chemical tests may show no presence of an antibody (the reaction that shows exposure) even though the virus has been present for as long as three months.

In effect, you can't be sure that someone who has a negative test to the HIV 1 virus does not have AIDS. After another ninety days the test should be repeated. Of course, you can skip the initial test if you stay with someone in a celibate relationship for ninety days and are sure that he or she is not being sexually active with other people. Then the test can be made with assurance of no exposure during that intervening ninety days.

A negative blood test should be taken seriously only after at least ninety days have passed. Some people go so far as to say one hundred twenty or one hundred eighty days would be better, but there's a limit to everything; you can wait a year and still not be one hundred percent sure. Ninety days seems a reasonable time and not too much to ask of someone who really cares about you.

What we are really talking about is a question of mutual trust and concern. That is, after all, at the core of any relationship. It should have paramount importance in dealing with those whom you love and with whom you expect to be intimate.

At this point in your dialogue with the other person, it probably will not be difficult to talk about blood tests since you have already gotten into the issue of AIDS, its spread, and the dangers present. Nevertheless, it might be helpful to have a few ideas as to how to deal with this discussion.

It is always better to take the blame yourself instead of giving it to other people when you want them to do something uncomfortable and difficult. For instance:

"I know it's hard for both of us to wait, and I find that I am very impatient about waiting the ninety days that all the doctors say is important."

Another way of putting it is:

"I can hardly wait until the ninety days are over, but I know it's just as important for you to be sure as it is for me."

The Bottom Line

When you boil it all down, there is no such thing as "safe sex." What we must deal with is the safest kind of sex and not the ultimate assurance that we all would like.

Even blood tests are subject to false negatives and false positives. A false positive is a test that indicates that someone has the antibodies when he or she does not. This can happen when a person has other viral infections. Repeated and more sophisticated tests can help to eliminate this possibility, especially if the person has no history of exposure and if no symptoms develop after a long period of time.

False negatives are a more serious problem because they can offer a false sense of security. One way of being more certain about a false negative is to repeat the test after ninety days. Even then, of course, another false negative is possible, but there comes a point of diminishing returns in everything.

The same kind of thinking is true about the use of condoms. It is true that condoms are the absolute best way we know now to have sex and keep it safe, but there is never a guarantee in life. The only way of being sure that you don't contract a venereal disease is not to have sex at all.

Even when you don't have sex, of course, you can get AIDS by other means of infection. They include blood-borne infection through cuts and abrasions from people who have AIDS and come in contact with you; blood transfusions; the use of needles used by other people; and accidental exposure. It is not likely that you can get AIDS from a toilet seat or an infected glass. The virus is very fragile and dies after exposure to the air or the outside environment. Even large concentrations of the virus can be killed by pouring liquid laundry bleach over them. This will actually destroy the virus completely. Of course, you can't use liquid bleach internally, you can't swallow it, and you can't bathe in it. But you can be sure that things that may be exposed, such as in laboratories or other places, are clean by using simple chlorine solutions.

Even boiling kills the virus. The AIDS virus is very fragile and will be killed with temperatures that boil water. As long as you go to restaurants where the glasses, china, and silverware are cleaned in the dishwasher, you are safe from the disease.

CHAPTER 3

How Does the Virus Kill?

W e have considered how to avoid contracting HIV 1 and HIV 2, the particular particles of organic material or protein that join together to form a virus. But why does a virus itself kill anyone? How can an organism so tiny that it cannot be seen with the most powerful microscope destroy human life?

Some viruses, such as the smallpox virus and the influenza virus, attack and kill by destroying certain cells in the body that render the victim unable to live. For instance, the rabies virus attacks the central nervous system and kills certain brain cells that are responsible for breathing or swallowing.

The polio virus can do the same thing and can attack the neurons in the spinal cord that are responsible for walking or even breathing. Other viruses, such as the ones that cause influenza, eventually can weaken the respiratory system so that the victim contracts pneumonia and dies for lack of oxygen.

All of these viruses are fought by the body's own internal

defense system. This system identifies the invading alien proteins called viruses and creates ways to attack them.

Our Own Defense System

The human body is a wondrous thing. The immune system that protects us against diseases is extremely effective, but a little complicated. It is important to understand the broad outlines of how it works if we are to protect ourselves against its breakdown.

Most blood cells are divided into two groups, white cells and red cells. The red blood cells are technically called erythrocytes. These microscopic disks appear in magnification to be like the wheels of a child's toy. They are round at the edges and thinner at the middle and when circulating in the blood appear to be rolling about. The red cells carry oxygen to all the body tissues. Billions and billions of erythrocytes circulate through the body. The substance called hemoglobin in their chemical composition is what causes the blood to be red in color.

The white cells are fewer in number but equally important. They have various shapes and appearances and are grayish white in color. These cells are the agents of our defense. Monocytes, lymphocytes, and granulocytes are varieties of white cells, and even among them there are many variations. Most important for our present consideration are the B cells that specifically attack and destroy viruses. These are the cells that make poisons called antibodies that go out and kill the virus. The B cells are actually tiny chemical factories that float in the blood among the red cells hunting foreign invaders. When one is detected the B cells create a chemical poison that attacks the specific enemy and destroys it. The weapons that the B cells use are related to the nature of the foreign substance. It would

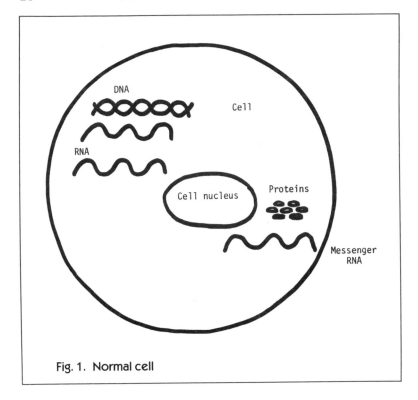

Fig. 1. Normal cell

not be useful if you were attacking a man in a suit of armor to shoot at him with an arrow that would bounce off his steel protection. Going into combat with an enemy armed with a shotgun when you have only a hunting knife would be fatal. The B cells have to determine what kind of weapon to use against the specific invader. For millions of years they have done so with great effectiveness. Only with the new understanding of the AIDS virus do we run into an enemy that is armed and dangerous and that the B cell is not able to destroy.

Each of us has an immune system in operation within our body. To make an analogy to a country under attack by an enemy, the body has an early warning radar detection

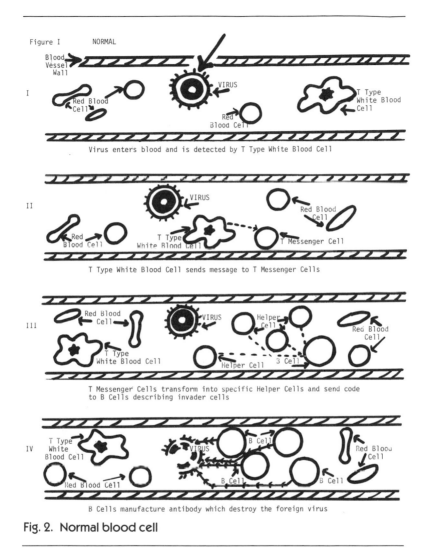

Figure I   NORMAL

I — Virus enters blood and is detected by T Type White Blood Cell

II — T Type White Blood Cell sends message to T Messenger Cells

III — T Messenger Cells transform into specific Helper Cells and send code to B Cells describing invader cells

IV — B Cells manufacture antibody which destroy the foreign virus

Fig. 2. Normal blood cell

system, just as we have for attack by enemy airplanes or missiles. The early warning system detects enemies on the way and about to invade our air space. In the same way the human body has an early warning system that goes into

action automatically. It consists of white blood cells called
T cells, which recognize the presence of foreign matter,
whether it be a germ or a virus. The T cells then give warning, just as the radar systems in Alaska or at the North Pole
do for the United States. The T cells send a message to the
immune system of the human body.

When the message is received from the T cells that a
particular agent has invaded, another mechanism called a T
helper cell informs the immune system of the actual structure of the invader. The T helper cells then code the genetic
makeup of the invading germ or virus and carry that information to still another part of the defense system. It is as
if the message were sent from the early warning radar
system to a central coding facility deep in the mountains of
Colorado. The warning system then alerts our defenses at
various airfields and missile bases around the country, allowing us to fight back. The T helper cells warn the B cells
by providing the structure and genetic code of the invader.
The B cells then create chemicals to destroy enemy germs,
toxins, or other foreign substances. The chemicals that B
cells make are called antibodies.

The body's system is extremely effective and in many
ways far superior to any radar alerting system in our
country or anywhere in the world. It has long served to
protect human beings against invading enemies whether
they be bacteria, fungi, or even wood splinters. The system
identifies the particular invader right down to the structure
of its molecules. This enables the body to formulate a specific poison to kill each invader whenever it appears. Even
later, if a similar substance attacks the body, the poisons
are in place to destroy the enemy.

In vaccination the body is challenged with a weak virus,
which stimulates the B cells to create antibodies to attack
that virus. Years later, if a similar but stronger virus pre-

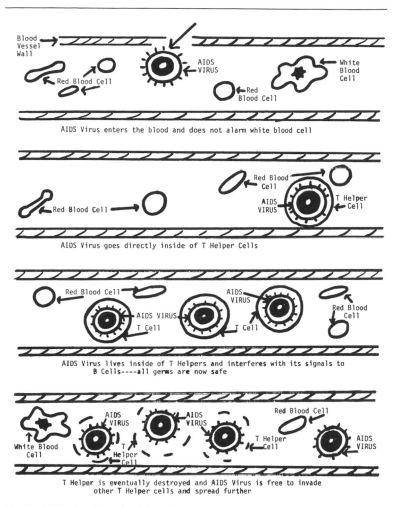

AIDS Virus enters the blood and does not alarm white blood cell

AIDS Virus goes directly inside of T Helper Cells

AIDS Virus lives inside of T Helpers and interferes with its signals to
B Cells----all germs are now safe

T Helper is eventually destroyed and AIDS Virus is free to invade
other T Helper cells and spread further

Fig. 3. AIDS virus invades blood

sents itself, the body is ready with the poison. The B cells
remember.

While the body is able to find antibodies to attack and
destroy smallpox and polio once it has been vaccinated
against them, it depends entirely upon the working of the

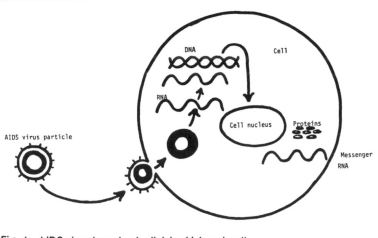

Fig. 4. AIDS virus invades individual blood cell

immune system. T cells warn T helper cells; T helper cells stimulate B cells; and B cells make antibodies.

Why Is AIDS Different?

Why is AIDS different from any other viral infection? Why can't we simply rely on our T cells, T helper cells, and B cells to destroy the AIDS virus? The problem is, of course, that the invader attacks the T cells themselves.

The warning system itself is the target of the invader. It is as if a brilliant enemy had destroyed all our early warning radar systems at once. By the time we know the attack is under way, we have already been vaporized. With AIDS it is even worse. Since the T cells are invaded and destroyed, there is no way to send a coding message via T helper cells to let us know what the enemy is like. The B cells are never brought into play. Antibodies are never made. The B cells

remain alive and able to respond, but they never are in-
formed where and what the enemy is. They become like
guided missiles to which no directional signal has been
sent. They are lethal but can't attack anyone. The onslaught
of the HIV 1 and 2 viruses knocks out our defenses before
they can be brought into play.

Eventually, if the AIDS virus kills enough T cells, the
human body becomes totally defenseless, open to every
kind of enemy agent. It could be a fungus, a simple germ,
or a virus that otherwise would be easily fought off. Infections that were only potential become real. Germs that
live on the skin and are usually harmless become deadly
invaders. All of our defenses are destroyed, and we can be
attacked and killed by innocuous germs.

Doctors call the infections that kill victims of AIDS
"opportunistic infections." That means that any germ hang-
ing around can take the opportunity to attack and destroy
the body because its defenses are not in place.

In World War II, when the Japanese navy attacked the
U.S. fleet at Pearl Harbor, we had no early warning system.
Our scout planes didn't go up to look for enemy ships. The
first moment that American armed forces knew they were
going to be attacked was when Japanese planes were bomb-
ing and strafing military and naval bases on the Hawaiian
Islands themselves. With no warning, no defense could be
put up. The entire Pacific Fleet was destroyed, as was most
of the Air Force. The same thing happens to human beings
who are without T cells. No warning is possible, and a mas-
sacre is the result.

A Case in Point

Sometimes people contract AIDS without knowing they
have the infection.

Wally A. was a twenty-four-year-old male artist who contracted AIDS but didn't realize it at first. It was early in our understanding of the disease. Wally didn't even know that such a disease as acquired immune deficiency syndrome existed. He was gay and had been involved for a year in homosexual lovemaking.

Wally began going to the hospital emergency room because of repeated colds. He thought that he was just unlucky in having frequent episodes of bronchitis and pneumonia. Doctors at first suspected that he might have diabetes, which sometimes first shows itself when a person seems unusually susceptible to diseases. He also seemed run-down and weak.

After repeated medical evaluations showed that he didn't have diabetes and there was no simple explanation for his illness, such as infectious mononucleosis (the kissing disease, or IM), the doctors began to suspect that something else was present. Eventually, when the HIV antibody test became available, it proved to be positive in Wally's case.

Wally was able to fight off a variety of infections over the next several months. The doctors would examine him, culture his blood or take samples of his sputum, and find out what germs were attacking him. They would then give him the right antibody to destroy that germ. Several times the medicines were able, after a long fight, to kill the germs. Wally's own body was unable to help.

In healthy people, antibiotics are used as supplemental fighters. The body's immune system does a lot of the work, but antibiotics help to paralyze the germs or prevent them from reproducing. This gives the immune system a little more time to build up levels of antibodies and eventually destroy the invader. If a person has no T cells, he can't make antibodies and has to depend entirely on external assistance. In Wally's case, this worked for a while, but he finally ran out of luck.

Eventually, Wally came down with a massive bronchial pneumonia. It was caused by a germ that had become immune to antibiotics. Some germs develop their own genetic system to overcome the effects of antibiotics and to live despite their presence. After months of desperate struggle, Wally finally contracted one of those germs. Efforts were made to support him with oxygen and intravenous fluids, but they didn't work. Wally died at twenty-six of a pneumonia that almost anyone without AIDS would have handled easily, perhaps without even becoming sick.

That is the tragedy of AIDS. Most of the victims are young and would have lived long and productive lives had they not contracted the illness. In the beginning most of the victims never even knew the name of the disease that was killing them. Today, even though we have a name for it, we still don't have a good treatment. Wally contracted it through venereal contact before anyone knew that such contact was even potentially dangerous. We know better now.

CHAPTER 4

How Does
AIDS Spread?

A s we have already described, AIDS is basically a venereal disease. It can be contracted not only through homosexual infection, as was suspected at the beginning of the epidemic, but also through hetero-sexual activity.

Because the AIDS virus attacks the T cells that live in the blood, the virus has an affinity for blood. At the beginning the disease is primarily an infection of the blood. Later it attacks the central nervous system, and the brain is often affected in later stages of the disease. Initially, however, and as far as modern scientific knowledge knows, it can only be contracted through blood exposure.

DANGER AREAS

Since the virus enters the circulatory system and there invades the T cells, certain specific areas of the body are most vulnerable to attack. These areas have the richest blood supply and therefore the greatest chance of exposing blood to the outside world. Such tissues are called mucous membranes. If you look at your lips or the inside of your cheek, you can see how thin the skin covering is and the underlying pink-reddish color that represents an ample blood supply.

Mucous membrane is also found in the nose, in the lining of the eyelids, over the eye, deep inside the ear, and in the anal and rectal areas. In women it is found in the vagina, and in both sexes in the lining of the urethra, the tube that leads from the bladder.

All of these areas, if they bleed, leave the person open to infection. Ordinarily, in the absence of AIDS virus, the body's defenses quickly come into play. The bleeding itself stimulates activity that causes a blood clot to form and heals the wound quickly. Tissue immediately begins to grow to cover the wound and make it once more a closed system, not open to the external air or to germs. If foreign invaders do enter the body, the T cells are called into action, and antibodies are made.

The problem with AIDS, of course, is that the virus attacks the T cells. If it is present near an open wound or bleeding, it enters the bloodstream and does its deadly work.

It is obvious that venereal infections are the most common cause of AIDS invasion. In heterosexual activity the vagina and the penis, both tissues lined with mucous membrane, are very susceptible to AIDS invasion. Any small tear or cut in these organs immediately allows the deadly germs to enter.

The vagina has an extremely rich blood supply. The cervix, the end part of the uterus, protrudes into the vagina. Because the cervix is exposed to the external environment during intercourse, any small erosion or tear on it can make a woman susceptible to infection. A cervical erosion is simply a small area of irritation on the surface of the cervix. It can be caused by almost anything and is frequently painless. It may not bleed much and therefore may be ignored. Nevertheless, it can be deadly if a few AIDS virus particles enter it; they reproduce, invade the T cells, and cause the destruction of the whole person.

Obviously, this danger is present only if the partner in sexual activity has the AIDS virus in his semen. The AIDS virus does exist in body fluids such as semen, sputum, and even tears, besides the blood.

Anal intercourse is extremely dangerous in males or females. The tissue of the rectum and anus is especially rich in blood, as is the vagina. It is very sensitive to any kind of erosion or trauma. The anus itself, the opening of the rectum, is very small and thus especially vulnerable to ripping or tearing. The anal sphincter, the muscle that controls the exit of waste matter, must close completely to avoid matter being pushed out when it is not supposed to be. Intrusion of objects larger than the size of a human finger can cause damage. Something the size of a penis or a hand or a fist is extremely dangerous. In sexual activity, it can cause the tearing of the mucous membrane around the anal opening and result, if the partner is infected, in immediate spread of the HIV virus.

Among gays, one form of sexual contact is the insertion of the penis of one male into the rectum of another. Occasionally they also use a hand or a fist to enter the other person's rectum. While this produces sexual stimulation, it can also cause great physical damage and, as we now know, ultimately a slow and horrible death.

It now seems evident that the initial infections of AIDS had to do with the ripping and tearing of anal tissue that occurred in homosexual lovemaking. Since the disease was first widely disseminated among gays, anal intercourse has

been determined to be the usual cause. Sexually active gay
men and women must be extremely careful about this
route of sexual gratification.

Less Obvious Causes

Since we know that AIDS is a blood-borne infection,
contact can occur in other ways that are less obvious but
equally dangerous.

The human bite is not a common method of infection;
nevertheless, it has to be considered. In the heat of passion
people can actually bite each other, even without thinking.
If the bite breaks the skin and the biter is infected, the
virus can be transmitted through saliva into the broken
skin and thereby into the circulatory system. People who
engage in sadomasochistic activities get pleasure out of
either receiving or giving pain. This pleasure is frequently
associated with sexual activity. Any kind of breaking of the
skin that involves contact with an infected person presents
a route of invasion for the enemy. This, of course, is true in
either heterosexual or homosexual activity.

Blood-borne infections also can be contracted in medical
settings. Doctors, nurses, dentists, and even optometrists
are potentially at risk. A doctor or dentist who operates on
a patient with AIDS infection is at risk. People who un-
knowingly carry the virus are like time bombs waiting to
explode. The surgeon who uses no gloves (especially dentists, who frequently operate without protective covering
on their hands) risk an accidental cut. The blood of the
patient then can enter the doctor's body and present another accidental but equally lethal spread of the germs.

Nurses who work in units where AIDS patients are
treated have been infected. Sometimes they may forget
sterile procedures and not wear gloves. If they have even a

small skin abrasion, that is, a tiny bruise, cut, or rawness of the skin, they are at great risk. Protective gloves are very important when coming into contact with a patient's blood through common circumstances such as taking blood in the morning in hospitals or even changing an IV infusion of dextrose and water.

The use of contaminated needles has been widely described in the press and the media in general. Drug addicts who exchange needles in the course of intravenous drug use take a risk every time they do so. The danger of other kinds of infection is always present, but use of a needle that someone who has the virus has used is in effect a form of suicide.

A Case in Point

Sally B. was a nurse working in a large general hospital. She worked in the emergency room and was effective in her job. She liked to help people in need, and she enjoyed the excitement and challenge that one encounters in life and death situations.

When patients come in under emergency conditions, it is not possible to get blood tests for diseases such as AIDS right away. Even if you do get the blood drawn, it takes time to have it analyzed and tested for antibody activity. When people have been in accidents or are in the grip of acute illness, there is no time to wait for the return of a blood test.

Sally was exposed to a patient who was brought to the hospital after an automobile accident. He was bleeding and needed emergency care to save his life. Sally was assisting the physician in tearing off the man's clothes to get a better look at the wound when she accidentally cut her hand on the scissors she was using. At first she didn't even notice the cut. She was already covered with blood and thought she had just pinched herself with the scissors. Later, after the emergency was over, she washed up and saw that she had cut herself below the thumb. Some time had gone by. She rinsed her hands and thought nothing of it. She didn't even bother to put a Band-Aid over the wound.

While the patient was recuperating, the results of his blood test came back: He had a positive AIDS titer. The way you determine the presence of AIDS in a person is to test whether the body has reacted to a foreign invader by creating some kind of response. Normally B cells create antibodies in response to an invading organism if the proper code is set up by T cells. In the course of the spreading AIDS infection, of course, the cells are invaded by the virus itself and are no longer able to give signals to make antibodies. None are available and the virus can establish itself, leaving the person exposed to any infection that comes along.

Sally eventually did develop a positive blood test. She now is awaiting the course of the disease in the hope that some medication not now available will prove effective to destroy the virus. In the meantime, she keeps careful watch on even small infections, and protects herself as best she can. She is not able to work in the emergency room anymore because she now has become a carrier.

The odds are relatively small for contraction of AIDS in a tiny area like a cut. Probably hundreds of nurses, doctors, and dental surgeons have been exposed to the virus and did not become infected. The problem is that once the virus is in the bloodstream a little infection becomes a great one. The disease, by its nature, continues to spread and multiply. The virus enters the body's T cells and eventually kills them. When a T cell dies it disintegrates, and the virus is left to float around and find a new host. It is like a parasite that invades a living organism. It invades the very nucleus of the cell and enters into the cell's genetic structure. It becomes part of the cell and does its deadly work in that manner.

Even small wounds should be taken seriously. If you discover that you have been cut and in contact with someone else's blood, the first thing to do is let the wound bleed for a while to wash away the potentially infectious material. Then you must treat the wound with a copious application of disinfectant. The AIDS virus is very fragile, and almost any disinfectant will kill it. Then consultation with a physician is imperative.

The kind of accidental exposure that Sally underwent is rare for most people, but it should be kept in mind and an effort made to take precautions always. Doctors, dentists, nurses, and anyone else who is exposed to people who are bleeding can be in a hazardous position. Protective measures are essential.

Another Example

Mary C. was a twenty-year-old high school dropout who had moved to the big city to seek her fortune. Unfortunately, she had no particular skills and very little education. She wound up becoming a prostitute and eventually became addicted to the use of heroin.

Mary started out by using the heroin nasally; that is, she would "snort" the powder in her nose to get high. That worked for a while, but then she was told that it was even better if you injected the heroin into the skin. She began getting hold of needles and syringes and learned how to cook up the powder by dissolving it in water and injecting it directly. She soon found that although she got high more easily by injecting the drug, scars and pockmarks were forming on her skin because of the contaminated materials contained in the powder that she bought on the streets.

Mary learned how to use the drug intravenously. She worked out a way to find the large veins on both of her arms and began injecting heroin regularly. Sometimes she would use it three, four, or five times a day. She got to the point where she needed to have the heroin all the time and couldn't wait for her next fix.

Mary was well hooked and unable to do without the drug. After a while she became so obsessed with the need to obtain the heroin that it was the most important thing in her life. She worked as a prostitute only to get money to pay for heroin. The fact that her procurer, or pimp, was also her supplier of heroin escaped her attention at the beginning. He was taking all the proceeds of her work in exchange for heroin and a place to sleep. She became totally dependent upon him as well as on the drug.

Soon all she cared about was getting the drug as often as she could, and she stopped even thinking about cleaning the needles or getting new ones. She didn't even bother cleaning the bulb that she used to suck up the material from the spoon in which she cooked it over a match flame.

It was inevitable that sooner or later she would use a contaminated needle. The needle could have been contaminated with a hepatitis virus, or the streptococcus germ that can cause bacterial infections of the heart valve, or even a simple staphylococcus infection that causes skin rashes. Her bad luck was that it was borrowed from a gay friend who had had AIDS for several months but didn't know it.

Mary used his needle one night when they were sharing some "scag" that he had gotten free from someone. She thought it was the luckiest thing that had happened to her that day. It was the most unfortunate thing that had happened in her short life.

A year later Mary began to develop a series of infections. She started to be sick all the time and to cough and be feverish. Mary contracted pneumonia at first and was treated for it. When the infections kept repeating themselves, doctors realized it was time to get a blood test for AIDS. The test was positive, and Mary was told about it.

Unfortunately, Mary had no other way to make a living than prostitution. Even though she knew she was a carrier of a deadly infection, she continued to ply her trade. Her pimp knew about the disease and made sure not to come into close contact with her, but that never prevented him from selling her to other men. The fact that he was selling a prostitute infected with AIDS didn't concern him.

Eventually, Mary became so sick that she could no longer work. Her pimp kicked her out, and she wound up a patient in a county hospital. One small piece of good fortune was that she contracted a form of pneumonia that caused her death to be painless and relatively quick, only about two years after she contracted the disease. Some of the young men who had bought her services may not be so lucky.

CHAPTER 5

Can I Be Infected?

At the beginning of the terrible onslaught of the AIDS infection in this country most people thought that they were safe from the disease. They looked upon it as the disease of "others."

The victims were said to be homosexuals or Haitians or drug addicts, all minority groups that most middle-class Americans felt had no relationship to them or their lives. They couldn't have been more wrong. Anyone can become a victim.

As we have seen, AIDS is a venereal infection and therefore can be contracted through sexual activity with an infected person. A person who has sexual intercourse with a known AIDS victim is at the greatest risk.

The most susceptible people are those who have frequent and regular sexual contact with an infected person. If that person is, for example, a gay male with a history of frequent anal sexual contact, the risk is the greatest.

As we have seen, people who frequent prostitutes are also at great risk. Many prostitutes have acquired AIDS through infected needles. A prostitute with the active virus in her blood has it also in all her body fluids. The AIDS virus lives inside of the T cells but is also found in body fluids where white blood cells sometimes gather. This includes saliva, tears, and the fluids found in the vaginal canal.

It is important to recognize that men are at somewhat less risk than women in heterosexual intercourse because of their physical makeup. The man enters and leaves the female's body in a relatively short time, so the exposure to the virus is short too. Even so, if a man has an abrasion or a sore on his penis or has been cut recently, he runs the risk of having infected body fluids come in contact with the wound and thereby give him the disease.

The admonition to use condoms becomes even more pertinent when you consider this kind of risk. Obviously, if you use a condom it acts as a barrier between you and the infected fluids even if there is a break in your skin.

It should be pointed out that there are homosexual prostitutes as well, who ply their trade in bathhouses and bars and on the streets. Because of their frequent multiple sexual contacts, they are a very high-risk group. Having sexual contact with a gay prostitute greatly increases the odds of exposure to AIDS. If you were playing Russian roulette, instead of having five empty cylinders and one bullet, you would be spinning a gun with five loaded cylinders and only one empty chamber. It is as close to suicide as you can get.

Safe Blood?

There are other routes by which AIDS can be contracted. We have all read about people who became victims through blood transfusions before the AIDS virus was detectable in blood samples. Currently all people who donate blood are asked to have a blood test for the virus. Obviously, if the blood test is positive, their blood cannot be used. The blood itself is treated to eliminate live virus anyway, and we are assured by the blood banks that the transfusion of blood is now ninety-nine percent safe.

Even though donated blood is ninety-nine percent safe, one more precaution you can take is to use your own blood if you know you are going to have elective surgery. In many cases a surgical procedure is done not in an emergency situation but because the doctors feel it is a wise thing to do. Such surgery can be scheduled a month or two in advance.

If you know you are going to have elective surgery or if a member of your family plans it, you might discuss with the doctor donating your own blood to the blood bank. It can then be frozen and stored and be available for you if it is needed during a surgical procedure. This is probably a good precaution for everyone, even if surgery is not planned. The blood can be stored for up to two years. If it is not needed you can replace it at regular intervals and always have three or four pints available in the event of an emergency. This eliminates not only the danger of contracting AIDS in a transfusion, but also hepatitis and any other blood-borne disorder and adverse reactions to foreign blood materials.

It must be emphasized as strongly as possible that donating blood carries no danger of infection. The needles used to draw the blood are brand-new and sterile and are discarded after use.

Who is Next?

Since AIDS first appeared in the Western Hemisphere among homosexuals, starting in the Caribbean area and then spreading throughout the United States, the initial reaction of most people was that they were safe if they were not gay. Anyone who thought the matter through, however, would recognize that it was only a matter of time before the disease spread from the gay to the straight population. A number of homosexual men describe themselves as bisexual; that is, they feel comfortable in both gay and straight activities and have intercourse with both men and women. It seems obvious that if they contacted men who had the AIDS virus and received it during anal intercourse, they in turn would become infected carriers. These men could then deposit the infection in the vagina of a female with whom they had intercourse at a later date.

It is very important to understand that the female, because she is the recipient of the sperm in which AIDS virus particles may be present, is at great risk. The vagina is an environment that does not destroy the virus. It is warm, moist, and protected from external danger to the virus such sunlight, high concentration of oxygen, and chemical exposure. The virus remains alive in the vagina and is available either to infect some other man or the woman herself if she has even the smallest break in the mucous membrane. Any small nick, even an irritation or a sore, could be its invasion route. Promiscuous heterosexual activity has become a most hazardous sport, and the players are an endangered species.

A Case in Point

Johnny D. was a 21-year-old college senior who admitted that he was bisexual. He came for psychiatric counseling, however, not because of his sexual interests, but because of depression. Johnny was extremely upset, frightened, and depressed. A few years ago he had had sexual contact with a gay friend. They had anal intercourse, and Johnny remembered penetrating his friend's rectum.

"He started to bleed. It wasn't the first time I had seen that. I knew that some gay guys bleed when they have intercourse.

"The guy didn't seem to mind, though. He was all excited and turned on, I guess, and maybe it didn't hurt him. Maybe he even liked things that hurt him, I don't know. There are some guys like that. Bleeding doesn't turn me on, but it didn't scare me either, at least not then.

"I'm scared now. I'm scared to death. This kid, I saw him a week ago. I was in the hospital to visit one of my friends on the AIDS ward. He wasn't doing so good, and I thought I would go and cheer him up. That's when I saw this other fella. I guess it doesn't hurt to mention his name. His name is Herb. Herb was there on the ward, and I knew right away why. He has AIDS, and he's dying from it. He looks awful. I went over and said hello to him, and he sort of smiled and looked at me in a funny way, and wanted to know how I was.

"It was like he was saying to me that I must have it too, because he remembers our contact.

"Is it true that if he has AIDS now he had it back then? Oh, my God, I'm scared. I'm even scared to get the blood test."

Many gay men who have had contact with AIDS victims and later see or hear about them become terrified. They tell me, and maybe they're right, "If I get the blood test and it's positive, I'll know I'm going to die. I like to think that it's going to be negative if I get it, but if I don't get it I can continue to think it's negative, and I'll be okay, I guess. If I do get it, it's like a death sentence. I don't know what I'd do then. I'm just not going to get the test."

Their concern is understandable. The problem, however, is that the only safe thing for the rest of the world is for them never again to have sexual contact with anyone.

Johnny had an even greater concern, that in the intervening three and a half years he had had sexual contacts with several women. He now thinks that not only has he become a potential victim, but also he may be responsible for the infection of several people. He's beginning to think of himself as a "typhoid Mary."

"I could be responsible for a whole epidemic just by myself, you know what I mean? I could be spreading the virus around. I had intercourse with three or four women over the past few years, and they were no virgins themselves. They probably have had intercourse with other men, and there it goes. It can spread just like dominoes falling. One knocks over the other. You've seen those things on TV. One domino goes down and thousands of them fall. I could be the first domino that's causing the whole world to fall apart."

Without question Johnny needed counseling. But he also needed to get a blood test. I wrote the order for him to get it at the lab so that we could be sure one way or the other.

Unfortunately, it turned out positive. At least, Johnny knows now that he should have no more sexual contacts. He has promised, not me, but himself, to abstain. He has promised not to be responsible for anyone else contracting this terrible disease. He is hopeful, as are thousands, that a treatment will be available before it is too late.

CHAPTER 6

Out of Africa

I t now appears that the original virus that gave rise to the current HIV 1 and HIV 2 infections around the world arose somewhere in central Africa. The concentration of acquired immune deficiency syndrome in certain African countries is far higher than anywhere else in the world, and it is widely spread among both men and women. In these areas AIDS is not primarily a disease of homosexuals or Haitians, drug addicts or blood recipients. It is a disease that is spread directly by venereal contact and that has become a major threat to the very survival of a vast number of people in these countries and possibly the entire area. Maybe the rest of the world is next. It is something we must consider.

According to our best understanding, the AIDS virus was long present in the green monkey of central Africa, which is native to the region.

Like all animals, including human beings, the green monkey carries a number of viral particles on and in its body. These particles are harmless to the species that carries them, but if they find their way into another biological system they are potentially dangerous.

It would appear that at some time a few years ago a green

monkey bit a human being and its HIV virus entered the human's bloodstream. The virus invaded a T cell in this person's body, and the person, whoever he or she was, became the first AIDS victim. He or she, before dying, had contact with other humans, and the disease began. Whether it was transmitted by heterosexual or homosexual relations doesn't really matter.

Existence of major diseases is not easily discovered nor reported in the depths of Africa. It wasn't until the disease reached the Caribbean Sea, around Haiti and later other Caribbean countries, that Western scientists became aware of it. At first it was believed to be confined to Haitians, and later it seemed to be found primarily in homosexuals. It wasn't long before drug addicts were added to the list, and so on.

Because of the great mobility of people in modern society, diseases spread easily these days as compared to ancient times.

In Columbus's day it took months to cross the ocean, and only then could a disease be spread by direct contact. Today someone can get on a plane in New York and be in Africa before the next day is over. Someone carrying a disease can easily transmit it before he even has a chance to be sick or even have a head cold. This is the way many of the influenza viruses have been circulating around the world in the past twenty or thirty years. The Asian flu, the Hong Kong flu, and the Taiwan flu are examples of how easy it is for a germ to originate in one continent and quickly spread to the rest of the world.

MUTATIONS

Viral particles are not actually living matter, but they have a genetic structure very similar to that of the nucleus of our human cells. The virus then can enter a cell, replace a portion of the cell's nucleus, and thereby alter the structure of that cell and kill it.

A similar mechanism seems to occur in some kinds of cancer. We cannot cure cancer yet, but headway is being made. Probably some relation will ultimately be found between the treatment for cancer and the disorder that we now call acquired immune deficiency syndrome.

The virus itself can change its genetic structure and the situations that it encounters. Originally we thought we were dealing with one AIDS virus and we called it HTLV III. Now we have identified another similar virus that spreads in the same way venereally. In order to conduct research more logically and efficiently, these viral particles have been renamed HIV 1 and HIV 2.

The two viruses now assume a similarity to the influenza viral infections we have described. We may run into HIV 3 and 4. The great danger would be if it became a droplet or respiratory infection that could be spread by kissing, sneezing, or using the same utensils. Right now that is not the case, but we have to remain alert. Germs and viral particles, bacteria and fungi are single-celled organisms. They don't think. They don't have ideas. They don't have purposes, nor even intend to hurt us. But they can kill us.

We are the organisms that think and work things though. It is up to us to protect ourselves against them. They are our enemy and we can destroy them, but we have to find the way to do it. In the meantime, our best defense is protection. The use of condoms has been discussed. The need for abstinence has been stressed, as has been the necessity for getting as much information as possible about any potential sexual partner.

Some experts feel that the spread of AIDS will encompass the entire world and that unless extreme care is taken, the virus can mutate even further, to become more easily spread and therefore fatal to even more people.

A Case in Point

Martha E. was a nineteen-year-old junior college student who consulted me recently. She was frightened and agitated.

Martha had been involved for about four years with an attractive young man of twenty-one. She had known him all through high school and into college. She told me, "Some people said he sometimes fooled around with other boys, but I didn't believe them. As long as I didn't ask to get married he kept paying attention to me. Why should I have killed the goose that lays the golden egg?"

As a result, Martha's contacts with other young men had been relatively few and far between. Most of the boys she met found that she wasn't really interested in involvement with them because of her continuing relationship with her long-time boyfriend, who was away at college.

As we talked, it was obvious that Martha indeed was agitated, upset, tremulous, and fearful. She was afraid, of course, that she had AIDS.

"I met Danny in high school when I was trying out for cheerleading. He was on the football team, a real all-American boy. He looked like Rob Lowe, tall, dark and handsome, and he had a personality to match. Charming, warm, a huge movie star smile. I went crazy about him. I guess it's fair to say I seduced him. We had a wonderful time. He went around with my group of friends. Every night, I went to his house to visit him, or he came to see me.

"Even though I was a virgin when we met, I knew that our sex experience was the greatest that anyone ever had.

I'll never forget it. Well, I guess I can't now, can I? You know what I mean. I mean, I found out that he died last month.

"Danny used to write me from college every week. Then the letters stopped for a few weeks.

About six days ago I got another letter. Danny said he had been sick, that he had a whole bunch of illnesses and problems, and that the doctors didn't know anything and were all stupid. He was sick all the time and losing weight, and nobody seemed to know what was the matter. He said he was afraid he might have cancer, and like that.

"I got this package Tuesday. It was from his college town, and I knew it was something that he sent me. I figured, well even though he's sick he remembered me after all. In the package were a few old pictures of us and a little charm and a note from some guy I never knew. He said that Danny was dead and that before he died he asked this fellow to send me the stuff in the package and to tell me that I was the best thing that ever happened to him."

At this point Martha started to cry. The tears rolled down her cheeks, and her whole body heaved with her sobs.

"Well, maybe I was, but he was the worst thing that ever happened to me, because the guy who wrote the note said Danny had died of AIDS. He probably gave it to me, too, don't you think?

"I mean, who the hell knew about AIDS a few years ago? I never thought I could get it. I never thought I'd have anything to do with AIDS people. I figured I was safe, I was above it all. I wasn't in any danger, all I was doing was having a little sex with a kid like myself. He was exciting, too. The best person I ever met, but not worth this.

"What can I do now?"

It was important for Martha to get a blood test as soon as

possible. Since it had been several months since her exposure to this man, we should have an answer as soon as the test was returned. If she had been exposed months back, she certainly would have a positive blood test now. If she had not, her blood would still be negative—unless, of course, she had been exposed to someone else in the interim.

She was fearful of having the test done and finding it was positive, but I insisted that it was in her own best interest to find out now once and for all, to get it over with, and to go on with her life.

Martha was lucky. The blood test was reported as non-reactive, meaning that she had no antibodies in her system at the time and certainly could not have had any from her dead friend.

Martha had dodged the bullet. Not everyone will be so lucky. You do not have to go to central Africa to contract AIDS. You can get it on a high school campus. But you do have to ask people if they will get a blood test if you will, and you do have to know something about the person you sleep with, aside from his looking like a Saturday afternoon hero.

CHAPTER 7

Is the Epidemic Really Bad?

A s this book is being written, and even more so by the time you read it, the disease AIDS will be far worse than it ever was. This kind of disease spreads geometrically. That is, if one person contracts it, he or she becomes the vehicle to spread it to more than one person in the future.

Scientists have devoted a great deal of time and effort to the problem of the spread of diseases and especially AIDS. Current statistics indicate that by the year 1991, not so very far from now, there will be a quarter million deaths from AIDS every year in the United States alone. Since the disease was first really spread in this country, even though it started elsewhere, we have a grim head start in the statistics. However, AIDS now has been detected in every western European country and even in the Soviet Union. It has been seen in Japan and probably is now being spread into China and the rest of Asia. It is widespread throughout Africa, through Central America, and without doubt will be seen in South America while this book is being printed.

Many scientists believe that by the year 2010, unless the disease becomes curable, the total number of deaths will reach one hundred million around the world. This is a staggering figure, one that is hard for the mind even to conceive.

What Can We Do About It?

Research on any disease seems to take forever. Even with diseases that are biologically clear-cut, such as high blood pressure, it takes a very long time for a medicine to be tested and followed up. The average length of time it takes for a major pharmaceutical company to invent, develop, and research a new drug for something as simple as hypertension ranges from five to seven years.

There are very good reasons for this. One of the main problems in drug research dealing with a disease that affects the whole human system is that any medicine that works has side effects. Side effects are the things that a powerful medicine does to people aside from the purpose for which it is used. Any medicine, no matter what its purpose, does many things to the complex mechanisms of the body. A medicine that lowers blood pressure can also cause rapid heartbeat, abnormal rhythms of the heart, dizziness, dry mouth, sleepiness, loss of sexual interest and drive, disintegration of white blood cells, and other things. Almost any new medicine is potentially the source of an allergy. There are people who have skin reactions to almost everything, including simple aspirin. Many drugs can cause bleeding, headaches, and asthma.

As you can see, almost any medication is filled with possibilities of things going wrong. Our bodies are so complex that it is very difficult to find one "magic bullet" to cure an illness and not do anything to the rest of the system. Even

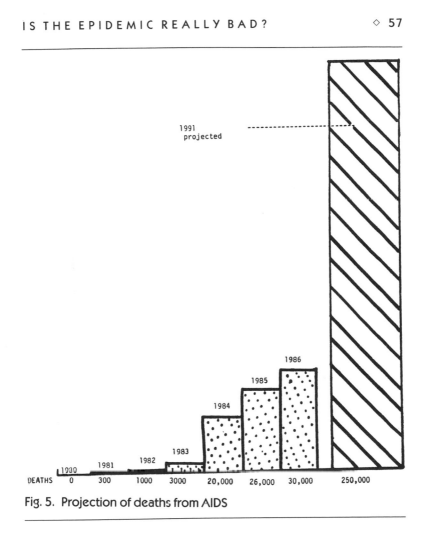

Fig. 5. Projection of deaths from AIDS

Ehrlich's "magic bullet," which was a breakthrough in the treatment of syphilis, caused many severe and painful side effects to the people who were treated; some of them felt that the cure was worse than the disease.

In dealing with AIDS we have a long way to go. No medicine has been discovered (to this day) that kills viruses by itself.

Since a virus is only a piece of protein that fits into the

chromosome structure of a cell, it has been necessary to kill the whole cell in order to destroy the virus. Obviously, a virus that totally invades the body and lives in all the cells is hard to attack. In attacking it, we attack ourselves. Unless someone comes up with a new method of attack against viral particles, we are indeed in for a long and painful siege in the next decade or two.

There is no doubt that the geniuses who work in scientific laboratories and who labor in hospitals and medical schools around the country and around the world will eventually find an answer. In the meantime, we have to fall back on some of the older answers that have worked in the past.

The only method of dealing with viral infections that has ever worked, aside from preventing them from entering our bodies, is to call into play our own immune system to defend us. This was the basic theory of vaccination, and it still holds. We have to find a way to immunize ourselves against AIDS, a disease that attacks our immune system.

Will Vaccination Work?

Vaccination has been our only major defense dating back to Jenner in the eighteenth century. It has worked over the years to fight off viral infection by building up our defenses in advance. Currently, we have to continue research on antiviral chemical treatment, and we shall do so, but while we wait for that we must fall back on the possibility of developing a vaccine.

To develop a vaccine, the first step is to isolate the virus itself. The chemical particles that cause the disease have to be identified in a laboratory and then grown in sufficient quantity to introduce them to animals that can develop a way to fight them.

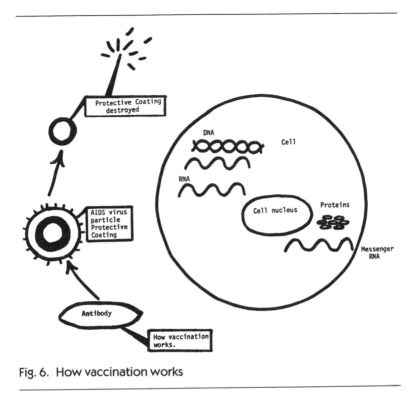

Fig. 6. How vaccination works

The first step has already been achieved. At the Centers for Disease Control in Atlanta, Georgia, the United States Public Health Service has succeeded in isolating the HIV 1 virus, and work is already in progress to grow the virus in a safe place. The virus can then be introduced into experimental animals whose immune systems will attack and destroy it. Most other animals, as far as we know, are not attacked by the AIDS virus. We already have the example of the green monkey, which carries the virus but does not seem to be affected by it. It is probable that chimpanzees or other members of the monkey family can be used to help us.

What scientists do is introduce the virus into the animal and allow its immune system to identify the virus for the B cells, which create antibodies to attack it. If these animals become immune to the disease, we will know that it is possible to deal with it.

HIV 1 is the kind of germ known as a retrovirus, which means that it grows slowly and can do its damage long after the disease is contracted. Because of this, it is essential to observe experimental animals for a long time before we know that they are indeed safe and not just harboring the virus until it finally attacks and kills them. In human beings the virus can exist for a number of years before it starts to do its deadly work.

If it finally appears that monkeys are indeed able to develop immune responses to the HIV 1 and HIV 2 viruses, then we must begin to experiment with the viral particles and vaccination in people. Even if it works in the monkeys, it doesn't necessarily work in us. Humans are different from other groups of animals, just as other groups of animals are different from one another. A disease that attacks cats does not attack dogs. Diseases that kill off giraffes do not necessarily destroy bears, and so on. Bacteria that affect apes do not hurt us, and vice versa.

It takes money to deal with diseases. The United States government has begun to appropriate funds to attack AIDS all out. Funds are needed to train personnel, provide facilities, and purchase supplies. All of these things are being undertaken. In the meantime we have to wait and try to buy some time.

In the Meantime

While we are waiting for a vaccine to be developed, we have to look around for other possibilities. Research has

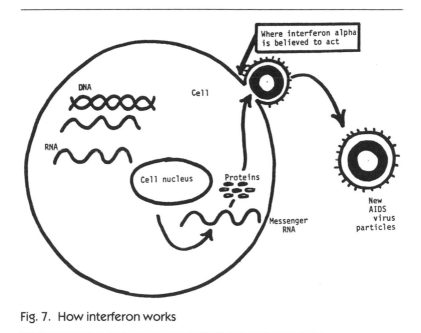

Fig. 7. How interferon works

gone on with specific antiviral agents that are found natu-
rally in humans and other animals. Drugs have in fact been
isolated in efforts to treat cancer or other virus diseases.
One of them is interferon, which has already been used in
AIDS research and in treatment of some AIDS patients. It
has serious side effects and frequently causes patients to be
quite sick when they take it. However, it has resulted in
small amounts of progress in some cases. Attempts persist
to purify it and find the specific active ingredient in its structure that can kill a virus. This avenue of attack will be ex-
plored intensively over the next few years.

Interleukin, another factor found in white blood cells, is
a chemical that attacks and destroys viral particles. It has
been difficult to isolate interleukin and to get it in sufficient
quantities to offer to patients having major viral infections

such as AIDS. That work is now going on, and research is beginning on the effects of this substance and similar ones.

Recently an agent called AZT has been researched and tested, and the Food and Drug Administration (FDA) has made efforts to speed up the final testing process to allow it to be used much sooner than is ordinarily permitted with new drugs. Apparently AZT has had some success in lengthening the life of the AIDS patient. It seems to act by shoring up the strength of the immune system. There is some possibility that it attacks the virus itself, although that seems less likely.

Even if AZT buys some time while other research is going on, it is worthwhile. Many patients believe that AZT has been helpful in reducing their symptoms, making them feel better, and giving them a chance to live long enough for a cure to be found. It is much like the old-time pioneers going west in covered wagons. When they were attacked by hostile Indians they circled their wagons and held off the Indians while waiting for the cavalry to come to their rescue. AIDS patients are circling their wagons, using interferon, interleukin, AZT, and whatever else may show up on the horizon to hold off the attackers until the cavalry can come to the rescue with a definitive treatment. A holding action is our best alternative right now, but help is on the way.

Quack Cures

While we wait for help, we have to be sure that the help is not a mirage. When people are lost in the desert and desperate for an oasis, the waves of heat that rise up in the desert sands sometimes cause visual distortions. The appearance of something unreal is called a mirage.

Many quacks are more than willing to take advantage of

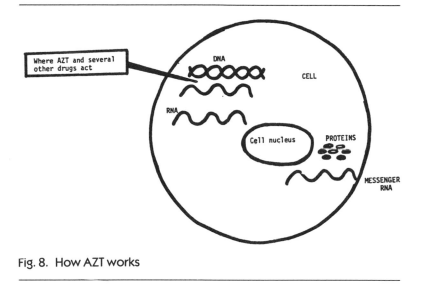

Fig. 8. How AZT works

people's desperation offering cures that do not exist. They indeed create a mirage for the victims of disease.

People have been taken in by phony cancer cures over the centuries. Unscrupulous quacks take vast sums of money from victims of disease to enrich themselves while promising a cure that never existed. The same thing is sure to happen with AIDS.

These medical charlatans try to convince people that the medical establishment has an answer but is holding it back. Sometimes they claim that they themselves have offered the answer to science but it has been rejected because of the power of the big drug companies or the greed of "the establishment," which they identify as the American Medical Association or medicine in general. Another ploy is to blame politicians or vague powers that are plotting against the welfare of the rest of us. All this is nonsense. If there ever were a major breakthrough in the cure of any life-threatening disease, everyone would know about it in

no time. The media is worldwide and penetrates everything. Presidents can't keep secrets from the newsmen. To
think that some doctor or group of doctors would be able
to keep secret a cure for a disease is ridiculous.

Actually, the opposite is the case. When new develop-
ments are in the beginning stages of research they show
some results, and the people who benefit from them have
to tell the world. Word gets out to the media, and premature
announcements are made. The demand for treatment becomes overwhelming, and it is difficult to convince victims
that much research must still go on, that the results are not
yet certain, and that there may be major side effects to the
treatment. The real danger is that word spreads too quickly,
and people have their hopes raised and destroyed within a
few days.

Case in Point

Arthur F. was a twenty-six-year-old hairdresser who had
been gay all his life. Arthur was happy in his profession and
with his life. He didn't think of himself as being different
from any of his friends, and he lived quietly with his lover
in a Palm Springs suburb. Business was good, and things
were going well.

Arthur would go out to a gay bar once in a while without
his lover and meet other people. The two had agreed that
this was okay on both sides. Art thought that a little social
activity mixed once in a while with some sexual game playing was perfectly acceptable. Later, when it turned out
that his lover had a negative blood test, he thought that was
how he contracted AIDS.

When Arthur started coming down with sore throats,
headaches, and general feelings of weakness and then

started to lose weight, he went to a specialist. He was told that he had a positive HIV 1 antibody test and was diagnosed as having ARC, an abbreviation for AIDS related complex.

Arthur was in and out of the hospital on a number of occasions, but because he had fairly good insurance and his lover had a good job they weren't in any major financial problem. They had some money put away, and they hoped that something would come along to change the grim picture that faced them.

One day Art met someone at a gay bar who told him that he had been to a clinic in Mexico where a cure for AIDS had been discovered. The fellow said that hundreds of Americans were going down there and getting cured. He went on to relate that the doctor in Mexico who had this special treatment had been prevented from using it in the United States because the big drug companies were hand in hand with the government and the FDA. These greedy people were trying to suppress his treatment because they didn't have the copyright on it and couldn't make the millions that they knew it would generate. The doctor told his patients that he was treating them almost at cost and made only a tiny profit to pay his salary. The treatment was expensive because it was so hard to make the medication, which was the product of the ground-up seeds of pomegranates, pumpkins, and other vegetation that had the ability to fight off the AIDS virus.

The idea sounded pretty good. What did they have to lose, a few dollars? Arthur and his lover got the name and address of the clinic in a border town in Mexico. It was only a few hours' drive from southern California and worth the effort, they thought.

They drove down, and Arthur started to undergo a series

of high colonic enemas, a special liquid diet of ground-up seeds, and some intravenous injections that at the beginning made him feel very energetic.

He didn't know that the doctor was giving him a combination of cortisone and stimulants that would make anyone feel good for a brief period of time. What effect it had on AIDS is hard to imagine, but the result was pretty clear.

Authur wound up spending all of his savings and those of his lover as well. In all, they gave the doctor in Mexico $39,000 and Art was no better. His disease continued to worsen, and finally he had to return to California, sicker, weaker, and more hopeless than ever. He was penniless and even had to sell his hairdressing shop to pay the rent.

Arthur finally died in an American hospital.

It is understandable to look for a magical cure when things seem the grimmest. If medical science can't offer a cure, maybe magic can. The trouble is that the magician's fee is too high and it can destroy the remainder of our life and security.

CHAPTER 8

Plagues of the Past

T he public concern with what we now know as an AIDS epidemic has parallels in the past. An epidemic occurred in Europe during the Middle Ages that was known as the "Black Death" or the "Black Plague," or simply the "Plague." It destroyed much of the population of Europe and Asia during the twelfth and thirteenth centuries.

The disease appeared suddenly and swept across the continents of Europe and Asia, killing as much as seventy-five percent of the population in major cities. It was so devastating that it created widespread superstition and panic. Some understanding of the Plague may be helpful in dealing with the disease of acquired immune deficiency syndrome, which has had a similar history and is terrorizing the modern world. Let's take an example of some fictitious people in a situation that may have well occurred in those day.

In 1183 Sir Gilles de LaTour, a knight-errant who had gone on a crusade to Palestine to rescue the shrines of Christendom from the infidel Saracens, returned home to Burgundy. LaTour, whose name means tower in his native

French, lived in a castle topped by a commanding five-story stone tower built by an ancestor who had been one of Charlemagne's knights.

Clustered around the base of the huge fortress were small houses inhabited by artisans, merchants, and certain members of the knight's household staff. Sir Gilles's lands, in turn, surrounded the village and were devoted to animal husbandry and the growing of grain and a remarkably good red wine grape. The grape and the excellent wine it yielded had become renowned throughout the entire Burgundian kingdom and in the rest of France as well. Wine purveyors from as far away as Paris sent wagons to purchase as many barrels as were available each year. Indeed, the income from the wine had financed the pilgrimage to Palestine for Sir Gilles, his fifty-eight men-at-arms, the horses and wagons, and his twenty personal servants.

Alas, the crusade itself had been far from successful. In truth, it was a dismal failure. Aside from failing to wrest the holy shrines and cities from the Saracens, the combined European forces were decimated both by battle injuries and illness. Strange diseases prevalent in the Middle East were unknown to the Europeans and wiped them out. Of the seventy-nine souls that had embarked that spring to cross the Mediterranean Sea, only thirty-one were able to return with Sir Gilles. The men-at-arms had almost all been afflicted by a strange and fatal fever. Those four or five soldiers who had been wounded in battle had been the first to die. They had been bedded down on straw pallets in the lower levels of a stone fortress built early during the holy wars. There wasn't much light, and the halls were damp, but it was better than being exposed to the heat of the desert sun. There were only a few rats down there and, of course, the fleas and lice that went with them.

The soldiers who had not been wounded in battle were

free of the fever at first. However, some of them had visited their wounded fellows in the fortress and they, too, eventually contracted the fever. As the number of the sick grew, Sir Gilles realized that it was time to go home. Not only had the crusade failed, but most of his men were ill and the rest had died. Supplies were dwindling, and the men were needed at home for the fall harvest.

The ship that had brought them to the holy land was waiting at the dock, and the noble crusader prepared to move his goods and men back to it. He himself had not contracted the fever, but he had never gone down to the lower levels of the tower to visit the sick and wounded. Sir Gilles had little to do with the men. He spent most of his time with other knights and noblemen, most of whom remained healthy.

Sir Gilles's supplies and wagons had to be returned home. Many of the animals were still alive and, of course, the remaining grain and other supplies were needed to feed the group as they crossed the sea.

Sir Gilles did not know, and probably would not have cared if he did, that there was a rat's nest in the bottom of one of his grain wagons. The female rat in the nest was, at the moment the wagon was being returned to the ship, giving birth to a small litter of offspring. Not only was she infected with the bacterium that we now call *Pasteurella pestis* but, of course, the fleas that infested her body had dipped into her blood enough to have acquired the germs themselves. It is the flea that actually carries the bacteria from the rat's blood to another source of blood, that is, a human being. It was the fleas from rats in the basement of the castle in Palestine that bit the soldiers. Thus began the infectious process that inflicted the Plague on the world.

As the vessel plied its way across the Mediterranean to the homeland, the baby rats grew. They were nourished by the grain in the wagons and were never detected. The fleas grew along with them and eventually began infesting the soldiers. In the Middle Ages, bathing and personal hygiene were never a high priority. Even the noblemen such as Sir Gilles rarely bathed, preferring to douse their bodies with perfumes to mask the odor. The men, of course, simply stank. By the time the ship arrived in Marseilles more than half the voyagers had contracted the Plague. Many had already died, and the survivors left as quickly as possible, considering it a "plague ship." No one knew how the disease was transmitted. No one suspected the rats or the fleas, or even paid much attention to them.

Of course, as the ship was unloaded and the wagons and foodstuffs were removed and the men left, so did the Plague carriers. The rats left the ship and spread about the docks and piers of Marseilles. Some even were able to remain in the food wagons and eventually arrived at Sir Gilles's home in Burgundy. It wasn't long, as you can imagine, before they spread throughout the castle and the surrounding buildings. The fleas multiplied along with their hosts and attacked the citizens of the town. Eventually, almost everyone became afflicted with the Plague, and this time Sir Gilles himself was included.

When the wine purveyors from Paris arrived to pick up their annual supply of the good red wine from the LaTour vineyards, only fifteen percent of the population of the town were still alive. Every other man, woman, and child had died. Very little wine was left either, but the merchants bought what there was.

In the course of conducting the transaction they came in contact with Sir Gilles's primary vintner, a man called Little Charles, or in French, Charles le Petit. Little Charles, who was fully six feet four and a robust and healthy man, had been bitten by a flea and had begun the course of the fever a few days earlier. In those days the disease was uniformly fatal. In Charles's case, however, in addition to his high fever and weakness, the infection had spread to his lymph nodes, causing painful swellings about his body, and had invaded his lungs. When this occurs the lung infection provides the opportunity for germs to be spread from man to man. That is, when a person coughs or sneezes, the germs are spread directly to others without needing contact with a flea. As the dying Little Charles negotiated with the wine vendors in his last act of loyalty to the late Sir Gilles, he coughed several times. The droplets from his cough were inhaled by one or two of the wine purveyors, who of course contracted the disease themselves.

By the time the germs had begun multiplying in their lungs and blood, the wine purveyors had returned to Paris. Once at home, they went about the business of selling their wares. They, too, of course, lived in houses filled with lice, vermin, and rats. In a few days the Plague bacillus was present in the rat population of all Paris. It spread about the city and eventually to the rest of France.

By a similar process, the germs were spread all over the continent and into Asia. Since no one was free of vermin in those days and hygiene was unknown, the illness afflicted all classes of the population, from peasants and serfs in the countryside to servants and artisans in the cities. It afflicted both the lords and ladies of the aristocracy and the merchants and bourgeois middle class of civilized Christendom. People died everywhere. By the time the disease burned itself out, it had killed almost three-quarters of the population of the known world.

The epidemic was probably the most destructive known to man since the time of the Biblical flood. Toward the end of the wildly spreading disease, people began to suspect that it was an affliction placed upon them by God. Sinfulness and evil were said to cause the disease. All kinds of superstitious ideas and reasons were found to explain the disease and its destruction. It was felt to be a visitation from Satan himself. Ultimately, no one was free from suspicion. Those afflicted were shunned.

When it became evident that a few abbeys and convents had been spared, it was thought that this was related to the protection of God. Actually, of course, it was because these people were totally isolated from the world and had thus avoided contact with the germ, the rats, the fleas, and the spittle of infected victims.

Years later a connection was made in the minds of some people that filth and dirt and vermin might be responsible for the Plague. This is probably the source of the story of the Pied Piper of Hamelin. If you remember, the Pied Piper was hired by the townspeople of Hamelin to rid them of rats by piping them out of town with a flute. When the rats were gone and the piper demanded payment, the townspeople tried to cheat him out of his fee. In revenge, he then piped the children out of town the same way he had done with the rats. Whether or not the story is true, there probably is some basis in fact that city dwellers in the Middle Ages began to destroy rats, knowing that somehow these animals were at the core of disease processes.

It was not until the end of the nineteenth century that science became aware of the presence of bacteria specifically and how the bacterium *Pasteurella pestis* causes Plague. It was not until years later that a specific treatment was available to kill the bacterium. Hygiene and bathing became crucial in avoiding the spread of the Plague, and they still are.

Other diseases and epidemics have had similar histories and have been controlled in similar ways. Malaria, which is spread by mosquitoes, was eventually conquered. Instead of finding a way to kill the organism that causes malaria, methods were devised to drain swamps and other breeding places of the mosquitoes that carried the parasite. when the mosquitoes were eliminated, the disease died out.

The AIDS Plague

With AIDS, science now has developed a theory. We understand how the disease is spread and know that it is caused by viruses HIV 1 and HIV 2. We know specifically how it is transmitted from human being to human being. We suspect it was originally caused by transmission from an animal.

AIDS is a transmitted by direct contact of blood, by neccles and transfusions, but primarily by venereal contact.

Venus is the Latin name for the Greek goddess of love, Aphrodite. When the Romans conquered Greece they adopted the Greek gods and gave them Latin names. Zeus became Jupiter; Hermes became Mercury; and Poseidon became Neptune. Many of the Latin and Greek names have become part of modern English. For example, an aphrodisiac is an agent that is supposed to stimulate sexual drive. Venus, in addition to being the name for the second planet from the sun, has also given us the name for diseases related to lovemaking, that is, venereal diseases. Webster defines venereal disease as "a contagious disease (as gonorrhea or syphilis) that is typically acquired in sexual intercourse."

Another venereal disease that has received wide attention of late is *Herpes genitalia*. There are many viruses in the Herpes family. Others cause diseases such as shingles and cold sores. Other venereal diseases are caused by tiny, single-called organisms called protozoans. Even fungal diseases can be transmitted venereally.

Gonorrhea is caused by a specific bacterium called the gonoccus, a tiny germ that grows in pairs and affects the bladder and urinary system as well as the sexual organs. At one time gonorrhea was transmitted from infected mothers to infants, just as AIDS is now. It caused irritation of the lining of the eyes and even blindness in newborn infants. This was controlled by the routine use of a solution that is still placed in the eyes of infants at birth. Gonorrhea was successfully treated after the discovery of penicillin. In recent years, however, the gonococcus has become resistant to penicillin, and other agents have had to be developed to kill this persistent germ.

Gonorrhea itself is spread by sexual intercourse, but it frequently remains in the womb of an infected female without causing her to have overwhelming illness. As a result, she can become the source of infection in men, especially if she is promiscuous. In a similar fashion the gonococcus can live in the prostate gland of men. If they are promiscuous they in turn spread the disease. Venereal diseases are especially pernicious because they can be spread by people who don't know they are infected. Sometimes, however, people who know they have a disease and don't care can infect others and not even tell their partners they are infected.

Syphilis is probably the best-known venereal infection and, curiously enough, it has a history similar to that of AIDS. Syphilis was unknown in Europe until after the discovery of America. It is now clear that it was brought back by sailors returning from the New World. Some say that it first appeared in Spain in 1493, and others that it was first reported in Florence, Italy, in 1497. In any case, the first clinical description of the disease now known as syphilis was written by an Italian doctor in 1497. By that time it had been spread in Spain by a sailor who had either returned from the New World and visited a number of ports in Europe, or had had contact with females in Spain who in turn had contact with others who then traveled to Italy. In either event, the disease became widespread in Spain and Italy and soon was rampant throughout Europe. At first, European countries blamed each other for the disease. The French called it the Italian disease, and the Italians called in the French pox. Others in Italy called it the Neapolitan disease if they didn't live in Naples. A variety of names were coined in other countries. In the same way that people in the Middle Ages blamed the Plague on evil spirits, people in the Renaissance began to blame syphilis on sexual excesses and, therefore, evil behavior.

There are other parallels between syphilis and AIDS. The first signs of syphilis are minimal: a small sore or lesion at the site of the infection; in the case of men, on the penis, and in women, in the vagina. The sore is not painful, and it disappears. Some time later a secondary stage begins with a generalized eruption of the skin and inflammation of the eyes, bones, liver, and heart. Sometimes even the central nervous system is affected. This is probably the eruption that was described in Florence in 1497.

The third, or tertiary, stage of syphilis is the most destructive. It causes tumors in the tissues of the body, especially the internal organs, the heart, and the aorta (the main blood vessel of the body), and destruction of the central nervous sysem. Lesions of the heart and aorta can cause aneurysms, or swellings of the blood vessel, which burst and cause death. When lesions occur in the brain they cause madness, or general paresis, a form of insanity in which the victim has delusions of grandeur. Depictions of insane people imagining that they are Napoleon or other figures of history were originally drawn from descriptions of patients with general paresis.

From 1493 until the end of the nineteenth century, almost four hundred years, there was no treatment for syphilis. Most victims eventually developed lesions of the aorta that ruptured, leading to death from massive bleeding. Others, perhaps less fortunate, suffered a lingering death from general paresis after being confined in insane asylums. It is said that Jack, the Ripper, the famous killer in London at the end of the nineteenth century, was actually a member of the royal family of Great Britain who had contracted syphilis. The lesion in his brain caused him to go mad and kill and mutilate women. It is doubtful that he realized his madness was related to a venereal disease; however, all his victims were women who he thought were prostitutes. He cut out their internal organs of reproduction, thereby earning his title of The Ripper. He was eventually captured and committed and diagnosed as having tertiary syphilis.

Soon afterward Ehrlich found his "magic bullet." By the end of World War II penicillin was widely distributed and had become the treatment of choice for syphilis. It still works, and we no longer see tertiary syphilis or general paresis.

Learning from the Past

As you can see, there are many precedents and parallels for our concern about AIDS. The disease has no early symptoms. It takes several years to develop. It can, and often does, spread to the central nervous system and cause a brain disease. Victims of the late stages of AIDS frequently suffer what doctors call dementia: They don't know who they are, where they are, or what is going on around them. The retrovirus has invaded their brain tissue and destroys it slowly but surely.

We must do everything we can to avoid the hysteria, superstition, and panic that accompanied both the Plague and syphilis when they first appeared. AIDS is not an intervention by God. It is not a punishment of humankind by some angry deity.

It is a disease. It is spread by a virus. It is nothing that we have not experienced and overcome in the past. If we can understand it, we can cope with it. There are no magical solutions, but there are reasonable, logical, and scientific things that can be done and that are being done. As mankind has done so many times in the past, it will prevail.

CHAPTER 9

Do We Have Time?

S ince the primary target of the AIDS virus is the human immune system, that is, the system that defends us against invading germs, we have to find ways to assist that system from the outside if we can't help it from within. Since we have not yet found an agent to kill the virus or to build up antibodies to attack it at its beginning, we need to find some other way around the problem.

There is a way to buy time. For the past fifty years we have had antibiotics to attack and destroy the germs that cause infectious diseases. If we can find the right antibiotic to attack each separate invading germ, we can kill it off before it does enough damage to an AIDS victim to threaten his or her life.

The problem we face is similar to that of children born with inherited immune deficiency disease, who live in plastic envelopes to protect them against germs. Obviously, not all AIDS victim can live in bubbles. We can, however, give them antibiotics to kill the germs that attack and take advantage of their weakened immune system.

Intensive work is under way in research labs all over the world developing new antibiotics. In this country, Europe, the Soviet Union, China, Japan, and elsewhere scientists are engaged in research to find new drugs to attack and destroy germs. Whole families of antibiotics are discovered each year.

The Core of the Problem

Because the human immune system is at the core of the difficulty, we must learn how to assist the immune system itself to work.

With the use of new genetic engineering techniques, scientists are learning many new things. Some very promising biological materials are on the horizon that seem to have the ability to stimulate the immune system and make it work more efficiently. If we can administer some of these agents at an early enough stage, before the AIDS virus has had an opportunity to enter too many T cells and before the human victim is weakened and unable to respond, we will be in a position to drive off the invader and defend ourselves.

That means, of course, that we must find people who are infected as early as possible. It is another good reason for regular blood testing if there is even a possibility of exposure through venereal contact, blood transfusion, needle prick, or accidental scrape in the vicinity of an AIDS victim.

If such discovery is made early enough, we can shore up and strengthen the immune system. Some of the early attempts at doing so were focused on interferon and interleukin. These agents are natural products of the immune system and seem to be chemicals produced by the white blood cells that attack alien viruses and germs. They are now being studied in clinical situations around the world.

Clinical research means using human beings in research projects. This is a long, arduous and very tricky matter. It is not done lightly, and one has to be extremely careful because of possible toxic effects of the medicine itself. Because of this, research takes a long time.

In research with interferon and interleukin, new clues have been found to even more sophisticated and complex chemicals. These, too, appear to offer promise from the very core of the immune system itself. Work with these has to be done in laboratories first and then in animals before human experimentation is possible. The problem is that all of this takes time. It will be several years before we have a clear answer on even interferon and interleukin.

What Can I Do Now?

One of the simplest things anyone can do right now is to stay as healthy as possible. Everyone knows that good health habits are essential in avoiding any disease, including AIDS.

If people keep themselves in good health, maintain good dietary habits, and avoid fatigue, they can often avoid contracting diseases. A regular routine of exercise is needed to keep in good condition. There is reason to believe that run-down people are more susceptible to diseases and less able to fight them off.

Such simple things as washing and keeping clean may seem silly, but the AIDS virus is extremely fragile. It can be killed by fresh air and sunshine. It can be destroyed by the chlorine in a pool. Such things as bathing with soap and water, always flushing toilets, and wearing clean clothes can avoid many diseases. We need to stay alert, eat well, keep clean, and be vigorous in our exercise habits to protect ourselves against illness.

Mind over Matter

Good mental health is just as important as good physical health. There is reason to believe that people who maintain a positive attitude actually avoid sickness. We know that people who think of themselves as ill eventually do become sick. These illnesses are called psychosomatic disorders. There is no question that people can psych themselves into being ill. Why can't they psych themselves into being well?

In a number of centers around the country people have experimented with using positive mental imagery to encourage physical health. Such diseases as cancer, leukemia, and others that have been thought to be fatal have been reported to be overcome by persons with a positive mental attitude. The person intensely believes that he can overcome anything. He is able to pull together all of his internal resources to destroy disease. "A sound mind in a sound body" is an old saying that still holds true. We have to maintain sound thinking and positive imagery in order to maintain our health. People who think well stay well, and people who think sick get sick.

Even persons who have already contracted AIDS and have a positive blood test can feel better through positive thinking while fighting off the disease with the help of antibiotics and supportive treatment from doctors. They can live in a more comfortable and productive way while they await science's efforts to cure them.

A Case in Point

George G. was a 32-year-old real estate broker stricken with AIDS. He was diagnosed after being plagued by a series of upper respiratory infections. He kept getting sick and going to his G.P. The doctor would give him medication and the illness would clear up for a while, but then something else would take its place. Finally, George told his physician that he was gay and wondered if he might have been exposed to AIDS. He had already changed his sexual habits by avoiding promiscuity and anal contact. He always used a condom whenever he had sex. Still, he thought maybe the damage had been done before he knew about these precautions.

His fears were all too well founded. He had, in fact, a positive AIDS test, and the reason for his recurrent infections became clear. His immune system was severely compromised, and he was unable to fight off the opportunistic infections that kept attacking his upper respiratory system and more recently his skin as well.

George had to be hospitalized on several occasions and while there was put in contact by the social worker with an AIDS support group.

AIDS support groups are composed of persons who themselves are afflicted with the disease and of members of their families, intimate friends and lovers, and others who are concerned with their welfare.

In George's case the support group helped him move toward a more positive attitude in dealing with his problems. He was encouraged to read a book by Gerald Jampolsky, *Love Is Letting Go of Fear*, which says in effect that if you can avoid fear and panic and despair you can take advantage of the positive forces in your own body to overcome negative ones.

That is not a new idea; it has been known for hundreds of years. But it does work. George felt it was worth giving a try. He also read *Anatomy of an Illness* by Norman Cousins. In this book, the world-famous author describes how he himself recovered from a severe illness through the power of laughter, warmth, love and even the possibly placebo effect of vitamin C. A placebo is a substance that a person believes will help him. It may be a vitamin or even a sugar pill. If the ill person believes it will work, it often does. George felt that this was a reasonable approach. He began taking vitamin C and following some of Cousins's advice. He started to watch video tapes of comedies and cartoons. He decided that anything that could make him laugh and be happy was worthwhile, and he felt better.

The basis of all this activity is self-healing. Self-healing has been known for centuries. The miracle is in the person's belief in himself and the fact that we all are far stronger than germs or viruses if only we can get our act together.

George had felt so bad about himself, his illness, and thinking he was on a downhill course that he became desperate to find something positive. He had to understand that positive thinking could make him feel good even if it didn't cure his illness.

He said in one of the group sessions, "I believe that everyone in the world is in the same position. That is, we're all floating around on the sea of life in a leaky lifeboat. We know that sooner or later the boat's going to sink and we're going to go under. We're all going to die. It's the trip that makes the difference While we're going around, there's nothing wrong with getting a bucket and starting to bail. The bailing gives you the illusion that you're making headway. At the same time, you're going someplace instead of waiting for the boat to sink. That's how I feel about taking the vitamins and watching the films, even doing some of the imagery that I've read about. It's something to do. It gives me hope. It's a positive attitude that's been missing from my life for too long."

Other members of the group talked about books that had a similar impact. They quoted from *You Can Heal Your Life* by Louise Hay of Santa Monica, California. Louise wrote that she had overcome vaginal cancer early in her life through her belief in self-healing and cleaning out her mind as well as her body. She felt that had helped her, and the members of the group agreed there was no harm in giving it a try.

Sometimes people feel guilty about having a disease even though they didn't ask for it and certainly don't deserve it. George said to the group on one occasion, "You know, I guess there are lots of people whose troubles begin inside themselves mentally before they even get sick. They feel guilty that they have a disease and somehow believe that they caused it, even when they didn't. I was that kind of person. I began punishing myself in my thoughts because I was sick. Instead of bailing out the lifeboat, I was punching more holes in the bottom. When I started to bail, I started to feel better. Watching Bugs Bunny and the Roadrunner, I started to laugh. The Three Stooges gave me the feeling that maybe there was something else in life besides feeling sorry for myself, and there really is."

On another occasion, George related a dream that he thought might help them understand how he felt. He said, "I dreamed that I was on a subway train in New York City. It was very much like a scene from a Woody Allen movie in which people are on two trains. Woody is on a train with a bunch of losers, people who are sad and unhappy, in a dirty, crumby kind of subway car. Across the platform he sees another train about to pull out of the station at the same time. It's filled with people in party dress, men in white tie and tails and women in attractive evening gowns. They're drinking champagne, laughing, and having a great time. Woody wants to get off his train and on the other so he can join that group. In the movie, both trains wind up their trips in the garbage dump; the party train and Woody's train full of depressive losers come to the same end point.

Well, in my dream it was different. I was in the car with the party group. I was wearing tails and a top hat like in the old Fred Astaire movies. I saw Woody Allen sitting in his train peering through the window and wanting to join me. I tried to get out and open the door, and I even told the conductor to hold the train so Woody could come and join us. It didn't matter if he didn't have a white tie, I told the conductor, just put him on the train. But the man said no, that it was too late. Our train was already moving. We were pulling out of the station. I finally decided, well it was too bad for Woody, he just didn't make it, but at least I ought to enjoy the party on my train. It moved out of the station, and we were in Switzerland going through the mountains. They were snow-capped and beautiful. There were valleys below with cows grazing on the lush green grass. I never felt so exhilarated in my life. I didn't want to think about where the train was going. I just wanted to enjoy the ride, and I did. That's about the end of the dream. I woke up without ever coming to the end of the trip. I'm going to keep enjoying that ride."

George went on to associate some of his thoughts to the dream. Since in the movie both Woody Allen and the people in the other train came to the same garbage dump, the symbolism was that everyone finally winds up at the end of the line of life and has to die. The real issue, George felt, was whether you could get on the train that was fun or had to be on the one that was grim and depressing. George decided that his dream meant he had finally taken the option to be on the right train and enjoy the ride.

This solution to coping with AIDS is not a bad one. Those of us who learn how to enjoy the ride can get a lot more out of life, whatever obstacles face us.

CHAPTER 10

How Can I
Cope with This?

A ll through our lives we face problems of one kind or another. Usually we can resolve them with reason or logic. Having enough information is one of the key ingredients. When we deal with emotional problems the same thing is true. Even when you are threatened with death from a fatal disease, such as AIDS or cancer, leukemia or heart disease, it is essential to cope. The emotional problems that arise under these conditions are serious and sometimes frightening. People often need help in dealing with them.

We have talked about group therapy and AIDS support groups, which can be of great help. Sometimes even more assistance is necessary. You may need to see a psychiatrist or psychologist, a mental health worker, or a counselor who can listen, understand what is happening, and offer some suggestions. This kind of help is called psychotherapy and is available through most high school and college counselors. If they are not able to handle the problem themselves, they know where help can be found.

When people become profoundly depressed, they need to resort to medication such as the new and effective anti-depressive and antianxiety preparations that are available through licensed physicians.

The psychological stresses that people undergo when they are threatened with death are extremely severe. That may also be true when members of their family are involved. When a loved one is afflicted with AIDS it can hurt you emotionally as much as it hurts him or her, and maybe more.

A Case in Point

Wanda H. is a 50-year-old, divorced real estate broker. She came for psychiatric counseling because she was confused and mixed up after having discovered that her son, Vinny, had been diagnosed as having AIDS.

Someone in the AIDS support group to which she first went for help suggested that she talk to the hospital psychiatrist because of the overwhelming intensity of her feelings.

On Mrs. H.'s first visit she seemed a well-dressed, well-groomed woman, within herself and comfortable in the office, not excessively upset. In fact, she expended a lot of effort to control her feelings. As she went on with her story, however, tears appeared in her eyes. They grew into full-sized drops as she went on. Every once in a while there was a catch in her throat. She would touch her handkerchief to the corners of her eyes as if to soak up all the gushing tears that would flow if she didn't go through the ritual.

"I guess I'm not the first parent to come here and talk about how heartsick they are about their children. I've met a lot of people whose kids have gone wrong. Some of them were drug addicts. A friend of mine has a daughter who's a prostitute. I always felt sorry for them, I guess, and probably looked down on them. I thought they had done something wrong and it was their fault that the kids got into trouble. I always felt that if you were okay yourself and raised your kids right, they'd be okay too. Well, something went wrong with Vinny. I know that now. I guess it's my fault, but I've got to do something to deal with it. He's sick and dying, and I don't know how to help him."

She went on to tell me that Vinny, now nineteen, was her only child.

"I was pretty late getting married, I guess. My career was always important to me. I started out in the real estate business as a secretary in a big office. After a few years I worked my way up and finally became a broker.

"I didn't have enough financing to set myself up well. Probably that's why I married Vinny's father. He was older, was divorced, and had some kids by his first marriage. He was in real estate too. We met from time to time at business meetings, struck up a friendship, and we got along. It seemed the right thing to do.

"Anyway, when we first got married I wasn't so sure I wanted to have children, but Vincent convinced me it would bring us closer together. Now I'm afraid it was a mistake. Maybe I knew it all along. He talked me into it, and when I was thirty-one I had the baby. We named him after his father. Instead of bringing us together, I think he pushed us further apart. I guess I resented Vincent for getting me pregnant in the first place. I was a career woman. I really didn't have time to take care of a baby, and he'd done this to me.

"Things got worse after that. By the time Vinny was three, his father and I separated. It wasn't the smartest thing to do, I know, having to run a one-parent household. But he was my child and I had to take care of him. His father used to come around and see Vinny every other weekend and take him places. Later on he married for the third time and offered to take Vinny in with his new wife. I wouldn't hear of it. Vinny was mine and always would be. Now I guess I'm going to lose him."

With this, Wanda began to sob. Her mascara ran, even the makeup on her cheeks got smudged. I let her go on for several minutes without interrupting. Finally, after the worst spasms were over, she continued:

"That cry is what I've needed for a long time. I needed to let myself go, I know. I guess coming here was my way of allowing it to happen. I've always tried to be a controlled person, you know, keep a stiff upper lip. We weren't supposed to show feelings when we were kids. We were supposed to hold them in and tough things out. Well, this thing is too much for me. I can't do it any longer, that's why I'm here. I'm depressed. I feel I've done something wrong. Somehow I've been responsible for Vinny's being sick."

Mrs. H. believed it was her fault that Vinny was gay in the first place. She felt that raising him without a father and spending a lot of her own time at work destroyed his life.

"He didn't have a role model, a man to model himself after, and I guess he modeled himself after me. Well, I wasn't such a bad model, I guess. Even before I met Vinny's father I was doing well. After I got his financial backing, I made it. I became the biggest real estate broker in this county. I still am when I can get enough strength to go down to the office and check things out. If I keep this up, though, the whole business will go down the drain, not that I care very much. It's the business that stood between me and my son.

"I'm afraid he wanted to be too much like me. Maybe he went too far. I knew when he was six or seven and wanted to play with my makeup it was wrong. I once caught him in my bedroom putting on rouge and lipstick. I thought it was cute. Maybe I even encouraged him. I guess I wanted to have a little girl, just like me, I don't know. All I know is everything's fallen apart."

It became clear that it was very important for Mrs. H. to get rid of her negative feelings. She had locked up all her tears and depression for too long. She had learned about her son's illness more than a year earlier. It didn't have a great impact on her at first, but in recent months she had become overwhelmed—especially so after Vinny's hospitalization with his final overwhelming infection.

"I was at the hospital today. He's got shingles now, that terrible infection. They tell me it's a virus, not the same as AIDS, but another one that attacks nerve endings. He's got huge sores and swellings all over his chest. He can't stand it; they have to give him narcotics. I looked at them, the sores, and I cried. I tried to kiss the sores. Isn't that crazy? It was as if he were three years old again and I was kissing a boo-boo that he got falling down. I'm not even sure I should be kissing him. They say I could catch it myself, or maybe I deserve to catch it. Can you catch AIDS by kissing people?"

I reassured Mrs. H. that there was no evidence at all that AIDS could be contracted by kissing unless you had sores in your own mouth. Even then, it was probably not too risky. Kissing and fondling and touching Vinny probably reassured him that she loved him.

"I'm glad you said that, because it's something I've felt a little strange about. I want to hold him and embrace him. I want to tell him how much I care, but at the same time I've had this fear in the back of my mind. I'm awfully selfish, aren't I? I probably held back a little today. I saw those sores and the pain, and I thought maybe if I kissed the boo-boo it'd go away. I must be really falling apart.

"I talked to Vincent upstate. He said whatever happened to Vinny was Vinny's responsibility. He was always angry at Vinny for being gay. I think he was mad at me, too, for not getting married again. We had a terrible time on the phone. We yelled and screamed at each other, just as we did before we divorced. He even accused me of killing Vinny. I guess that was the last straw. I just hung up on him. I didn't know what else to do."

Wanda went on to talk about her plans for the future. They were ominous.

"I've thought about taking care of Vinny and trying to make him as comfortable as possible. I want him to have as much medication as possible to stop the pain and unhappiness. Maybe I'll even save some of those pills and store them away. When he dies I could go along with him and comfort him in the hereafter, if there is such a thing. After all, if I did it to him, I guess I ought to be punished, too."

I was concerned about Wanda's formulating a suicide plan in her mind. Some of her ideas were typical of a profoundly depressed person. The fact that she had let go the flood of tears had been helpful, but it showed how severe her feelings really were.

I tried to reassure Wanda that being gay was not a disease, nor something that anyone had caused to happen. I told her that even the American Psychiatric Association, which at one time regarded homosexuality as a disease, no longer classifies it that way. It is now considered another life-style, a matter of choice. I thought that maybe this would relieve her guilt, and it seemed to help a little. She went on:

"Well, I know you're trying to make me feel better. After all, that's what you're supposed to do, isn't it? I guess there's something in what you say, but I can't help thinking that at the core of it all it's still my fault. Somehow I did it. I know it. I helped, or I made, or somehow I caused Vinny to get this disease."

I urged that Mrs. H. come in as often as possible to see if we could deal with some of these terrible feelings before they got worse. I also prescribed some antidepressant medication, and I gave her some to take before she left the office. I told her it would give her some additional strength and mental energy to help her get through the difficult time that faced her. After all, her son's illness could go on for a long time. She agreed to try the medication and made a series of appointments for the next few weeks.

Over the course of Wanda's subsequent visits, we talked about AIDS and how to understand it better. I told her it was conceited on her part to assume that she was the one who created her son's whole personality, life-style, or even sexual preference. Not even the strongest mother has that much influence over her son. I also suggested that she try to reconcile with Vinny's father so that he might have a more positive attitude toward his son at this crucial time. Maybe that would help Vinny too.

She said, "I know Vincent is mad at me. He thinks I just used him to get going in the real estate business and then dumped him. But I guess there might be some way for me to talk to him. We've never really been close, even at the beginning, but for Vinny's sake, I'll try. I'll call him tonight. I'll tell him that I've been seeing you and that you suggested we talk. Maybe it'll help, what've I got to lose? I'll do anything I can to help Vinny. If you think it would help to have his father come down, I'll try."

She followed my advice and was surprised to find that her ex-husband really was concerned. Vinny was his only son and his namesake. He had somehow hoped that the boy might follow in his footsteps. When he lost him in the divorce and realized that he had no influence over him, he became angry at his ex-wife and his son, too. He later told Wanda that he had taken out his own problems on her and their son. He agreed to come down and visit.

At her next appointment Wanda reported, "You could have knocked me over with a feather when Vincent told me he was to blame, too. I guess I always suspected that it was true, but he really surprised me. We went over to the little bar across the street from the hospital. We both felt we needed a drink to fortify ourselves before seeing Vinny. He's got a urinary tract infection now. The shingles are better, but now he's got this bug in his bladder. He has a fever, and he looks terrible. They don't seem to be able to find the right combination of medicines to kill the germs. I guess that's part of the disease, isn't it, Doctor?

"Well, anyway, we sat there and talked, his father and I. He even took my hand and squeezed it. For a moment I was sorry I ever divorced him. Well, it's too late now. But at least we got things straightened out about Vinny. His dad sat with him, and Vinny was so happy to see him. Vincent didn't talk about being mad at him, about being gay or being bad. They just were able to talk like a father and son should. His father's got some love inside of him. I'm glad I got him to show it."

It wasn't much later in the course of Wanda's treatment that her son died. He had been on a rapid downhill course, unable to fight off intermittent infections. Vinny died in the hospital, and his parents agreed to have him buried in his father's family plot.

Wanda became resigned to the outcome. "I guess working with you has helped me more than I can say. I really don't feel that I killed Vinny, any more than if he had caught typhoid or been hit by a car. It's something that happens in life. Now that my only child is gone, I'm going to have to deal with it. I'm going to go on and cope with my life. I guess we all have to do that. I've thought a lot about it, and I've decided maybe I could do something for others too. There are the AIDS groups and the AIDS Center. I could go down there and help them. I'm pretty good at organizing things—some people think too good. They say I'm always trying to be in charge. Well, this is something that needs all the help it can get.

"I'm going to try. Don't worry, I'm not going to take all those pills that I saved up. I flushed them down the toilet. I didn't flush the antidepressant pills, though. I think they're helping me. I do feel better. I'm sleeping better. My appetite's back. I have more energy. I can take that energy and use it for something good instead of wailing and crying."

Wanda was typical of a number of parents of young people who develop AIDS. They have mixed feelings. On the one hand, they're angry at their children for getting sick in the first place, but on the other they blame themselves. They think they're the cause of all the trouble. Of course, none of that is true.

Many parents feel responsible for everything their children do long after they grow up. As Wanda pointed out, there are parents who feel that if their children get typhoid or are killed by an auto, they are still to blame. Somehow they should have advised the child not to cross the street when the car was coming. They assume responsibility as if the children were still infants. It is part of the task of parents to allow their children to grow away from them and to become independent. If they cannot do that, it hurts both sides.

Wanda's inability to see that her son was a separate person damaged him as he grew up. People who do not achieve independence from their parents and become able to do things on their own come to feel inadequate. That doesn't help in making good choices in adult life.

It was too late for Vinny to benefit from his mother's ability to understand that he was separate, but it wasn't too late for Wanda H. to be free of guilt and to cope with the overwhelming tragedy of her son's death.

CHAPTER 11

An Ounce of Prevention

We don't have even an ounce of cure, much less a pound, at this time in our understanding of acquired immune deficiency syndrome. The only thing we do have is prevention. We know that AIDS is primarily a venereal disease. With the exception of blood-borne contact, which is discussed later in the chapter, the major source of the virus is through sexual contact. Obviously, the foolproof way of preventing spread of the disease is celibacy. Total avoidance of sex would eliminate the greatest possibility for contact with the virus.

Since it is unlikely that people will totally avoid sex, we have to make sex as safe as possible. The first step is to eliminate as much risk as we can. That is done through checking out your sexual partners. The days of promiscuous sex should be over. It is dangerous to have sexual relations with someone whom you don't know.

Sexual activity can be a beautiful and fulfilling part of anyone's life. We all have instinctive drives that lead us into sex. The continuation of human life is totally dependent upon reproduction. What we have to do is to control our instinctive drives and channel them in the best way we can.

There are many myths about AIDS that need to be dispelled as well. You cannot get AIDS from exposure to improperly washed glasses in restaurants or spoons or forks in someone's house. It cannot be transmitted by sneezing or by the use of sanitary facilities such as toilet seats. It is important to maintain good safety habits and hygiene to avoid illness in general, but that is not a factor as far as AIDS is concerned. People have been frightened of going to restaurants operated by gays or staffed by waiters or waitresses who may be homosexual. This is part of a general hysteria similar to that found in accounts of the Plague centuries ago. It belongs in the Middle Ages and not in modern times.

But I'm Scared to Death!

The advent of AIDS has given rise to a new phobia. Phobias are unrealistic fears. People are afraid of heights and airplanes, buses, trains, and public meetings. Others are fearful of snakes, rats, insects, and even people. Most psychoanalysts believe that phobias are displaced fears from other things, usually having to do with sex, power, and control. That is, people who can't handle their instinctive sexual drives substitute the fear of sexual contact for a fear, for example, of snakes or mice. Something that crawls or runs up your leg, or might do so, relates to the sexual organs and the fear of having them touched. Doctors are able to help patients deal with phobic problems. Self-help groups around the country, similar to Alcoholics Anonymous, help frightened people to help themselves.

Some people are fearful of losing control and letting

things overcome them from inside. Instead of dealing with the direct fear of their own power or their own unconscious needs, they turn those fears around and become afraid of outside things. They become afraid of other people in groups or even individually, of walking on the street or getting into an airplane, a subway, or a bus. This kind of fear is displaced from the fear of loss of control, and can be dealt with. Doctors have found mild tranquilizers very helpful in treating panic. Some of the antidepressants have been useful too.

Doctors also encounter disease phobias. Sufferers worry that they will develop cancer and keep feeling their bodies for lumps and bumps in unlikely places. Or they fear heart disease and constantly go to doctors to have cardiograms, incessantly take their own pulse, and even buy a stethoscope to listen to their own heartbeat.

It is important to have regular medical checkups to rule out the possibility of disease, but an overwhelming fear can interfere with one's life and waste time, energy, and lots of money as well.

The kind of phobia that people develop depends first of all upon the degree of their fear about loss of control. They don't feel good about themselves or strong enough inside to cope. AIDS provides an obvious new focus for such fear.

People over the years have been phobic about sex. A person can be intimidated by any kind of sexual interest, fearing that in some way it will allow others to get too close or that the person will lose control. This fear of intimacy is a major emotional problem and needs to be dealt with by a professional.

Isn't Sex Dangerous?

Historically, both men and women have avoided sex and intimacy because they said they were afraid of venereal disease. Syphilis and gonorrhea are indeed dangerous enemies, but for most of this century we have had treatment for both infections. Nevertheless some people still use this kind of thinking to rationalize away their fear of sex and avoid it entirely. An AIDS phobia has come to the fore as the latest manifestation of this disorder.

The use of precautions, the avoidance of inappropriate partners, and the use of condoms are a form of insurance. Using a condom is buying insurance against AIDS and other venereal diseases as well. Sex is necessary to continue life. What we must do is make it as safe as possible, but not avoid it entirely.

A Case in Point

Mary J. was a nineteen-year-old junior college student who applied to a convent for admission as a novice.

Many young women decide that their vocation in life is to work for God. This is a positive and useful career. Sometimes, however, people seek the church as a refuge from living their own lives.

Mary went through the usual process of interviews and psychological tests that modern churches use to screen applicants.

The Mother Superior at the convent was concerned about Mary especially because she wasn't a member of that religion. She had decided to enter the convent, she said, because she wanted to convert and also because she knew this was the only way she could live her life. The psychological tests indicated that Mary had many areas of insecurity and that professional counseling should be considered before she was accepted as a novice.

It was Mary's first interview with a psychiatrist. She had taken some tests and met psychologists in school but had never encountered a psychiatrist before. She said, "Psychiatrists are for really crazy people, aren't they?"

It took me some time to convince her that many people consult psychiatrists because of problems in living or issues that they haven't quite resolved. They are far from crazy. I tried to reassure her that no one thought she was insane. The real intent was to find out if some of the things going on inside her might not be related to her choice of religion as a career.

It turned out that Mary was full of fear. She was fearful of getting close to people in the first place. She had never really felt strong about herself and believed she was unattractive, even ugly. She had never dated. In fact, when boys talked to her she would screw up her face as if she had been sucking a lemon and look down at the ground. After a while people stopped even trying to have conversations with her. She had very few girl friends because she didn't feel comfortable talking with them. "They're always talking about boys and dates and all the material things of life. They aren't spiritual like me," she said.

Mary truly was a person who had a phobia in the making. When AIDS first broke on the scene, she was sure it was God's punishment on the world for all its sinning. Any kind of sexual activity was taboo, and AIDS was the price that the human race was paying for it. She was convinced of this, and decided that retreat into a convent was the best way to avoid punishment.

Since religious orders do not want people who have major emotional problems or whose commitment to God is related more to negative factors than positive, Mary was not accepted. We discussed this at great length. Eventually she decided to enter a long-term course of psychotherapy. She stayed at college and gradually began to have a better view of herself.

Mary now has transferred to a four-year university. She now thinks she is reasonably attractive and is dressing the part. She has joined some clubs and special interest groups and takes part in their meetings and discussions along with the other kids. She can talk to boys now, and while still uncomfortable about the prospect of dating, she is considering it. She plans to continue with psychological counseling and hopes to deal with life in a more realistic way in the future.

NONSEXUAL AIDS CONTACT

We have talked about how AIDS can be transmitted by blood. At the beginning of the AIDS epidemic, we were not even aware that a virus was involved. There were some blood donors who had AIDS and transmitted it to unknowing recipients. The doctors and the nurses did not know, nor did the patients. We understand that problem now, and have taken steps in blood banks all around the world to prevent the transmission of AIDS by this method.

Most blood banks now assert that ninety-nine percent of the blood that they store is safe. There is always a one percent chance of something going wrong, but that's true in almost everything in life.

People who received blood five, six, or seven years ago and have not come down with any infection are probably safe now. Those who received transfusions since the AIDS disease became known and before blood testing was possible are at risk and probably should have a blood test to reassure themselves.

One supersafe way of receiving blood is to use your own

blood. Before elective surgery you can donate your own blood to the blood bank, have it stored there, and avoid any possibility of getting a disease from strange blood. To cope with emergencies, it is possible in some communities to donate blood and leave it in storage; then by giving at regular intervals of, say, six months, you can always have three or four pints available.

Of course, you can't get AIDS by giving blood. The needles used to withdraw the blood are brand-new and are discarded after use. Giving blood is safe.

Even drug addicts are becoming aware of the danger of AIDS. In their desperation for drugs to ease their deep craving and unresolved emotional problems, they used to use anything to stick into their blood vessels. They used other people's needles without even bothering to wash them. The high incidence of AIDS among prostitutes is largely a result of needle contact. Since many prostitutes are also narcotic addicts and share their needles and supplies with their friends, you can see how quickly the disease can be spread.

Efforts are being made to educate drug addicts, along with everyone else, about the transmission of disease by intravenous injection or even by "skin popping." While there is never an excuse for drug addiction, at least those addicts who are unable to rid themselves of the disease can avoid a permanent cure for it through AIDS by being sure their needles are clean.

There are ways to deal with drug addiction. They are painful emotionally and take a long, long time. But most agree it's better to try to overcome the addiction than to die as a side effect of the habit.

CHAPTER 12

The Future Is in Our Hands

One of the things that distinguish human beings from the other inhabitants of our planet has been our ability to look to the future and deal with it in our own best interest. Now that we are faced with a major threat to our existence, and recognize it as such, we have begun to take up the challenge.

Research programs are going forward all around the world. In the United States, major funds have been allocated to the effort. A crash program similar to those used to develop the atomic bomb and to send men into space is being put in place. Researchers from universities, hospitals, federal facilities, and private groups have been asked to help. There is hope for the future. We will overcome this problem. The more knowledge we have about anything, the more we are able to cope with it. The more we know, the more we can do.

Knowledge about AIDS can help us to learn more about the system that it attacks. The immune system is, as we have seen, the most important one in our bodies to protect us from the environment in which we live. Through the research going on now, we will learn more and more about infectious agents and invaders that might come in the future. Who knows, someday we might have to deal with organisms and life forms from star systems elsewhere in the universe. The research we are doing now can pay dividends for untold future generations.

Even at this time, study of the immune system can be of tremendous value. All around the world methods are being developed to transplant organs from donors to people whose bodies are not functioning well. Kidney and liver transplants have been successfully performed for a decade. Heart transplants are beginning to come to the fore and may provide an answer to chronic and overwhelming heart disease for many young people. One of the problems with transplants has been that the immune system rejects foreign invaders. That, of course, is what it is supposed to do. But when we introduce a foreign substance such as a liver or a kidney, the body reacts as if it were an invader, even though its entry has a benign purpose.

Research into the workings of the immune system is essential to success in accomplishing transplants. It may make it possible for thousands of people to live who would otherwise perish because their bodies reject donor organs.

An Unexpected Dividend

In addition to leads that we may get concerning the acquired immune deficiency syndrome viruses HIV 1 and HIV2, we are also learning more about other workings of the immune system. It seems likely now that cancer, mankind's oldest and most implacble enemy, is intimately related to viral infections. Several types of cancer have already proved to be due to viruses. It may well be that the workings of the immune system and how it deals with invaders has something to do with triggering cancer-causing mechanisms in the body. We have even seen situations in which cancer seems to have been triggered by AIDS. There is a relationship. It may be that if we can cure AIDS, we will also take a giant step forward in our understanding of cancer.

The programs will go on. Research will be encouraged, not only here, but all over the world. All of us have a stake in destroying this enemy. The problem now is to avoid panic, phobias, and terror about the disease.

In the United States two hundred years ago people were terrorized by the notion that witches and demons afflicted certain people. These people were tried and condemned as witches and burned at the stake. The most famous of these were the trials in Salem, Massachusetts, but the same kind of thinking went on across the country and, indeed, across the world in those days. It was a product of the hysteria of the Middle Ages. Superstition and fear of people who were different were at its root.

A new witch hunt is possible in dealing with AIDS. Some people feel that the original victims of AIDS—prostitutes, gays, people from the Caribbean islands, and drug addicts—are weird, despicable, different, and somehow evil.

People have said that AIDS is a punishment from God. If it is, it now promises to afflict all of us. God is not discriminating against "out" groups. We must avoid hysteria and panic. We must not allow the phobic preoccupation with AIDS to allow us to push away those of our fellow human beings who are different from us.

AIDS, like so many other things, is a process, a disease entity, a system of biological activity that we have not yet completely understood. It is not magic. It is not mystical. It is not a religious issue. It is a medical problem. It has social and emotional effects. It can be a psychological and psychiatric problem. But it can be handled. Anything that human beings encounter can be handled, has been handled, and will be handled.

Therefore, when we deal with fellow human beings who may be afflicted with AIDS, or read about them in the paper, we have to assume that the problem has something to do with us. As John Donne told us centuries ago, when you hear the sound of a church bell tolling the death of another person:

"...never send to know for whom the bell tolls; it tolls for thee."

CHAPTER 13

AIDS Q and A

Here are a series of questions frequently asked concerning AIDS. See how many of them you can answer.

Q: Can you get AIDS from kissing?

A: It is highly unlikely that you can get AIDS from ordinary kissing. Theoretically it can happen if there is a wound or lesion in your mouth. If that is the case, you shouldn't be kissing in the first place. Usually, swallowing small quantities of saliva or having it in your mouth will not result in AIDS or any other disease.

Q: Can you get AIDS from oral sex or swallowing semen?

A: No. As long as there is no trauma or injury inside the mouth, with blood being exchanged, the same answer is true of semen as of kissing.

Q: Can women get AIDS by having sex with other women?

A: Yes. If a person is infected by the virus, that person's blood and the secretions of her cervix and vagina are contagious as well. Therefore, there can be exposure to the virus. However, the usual kind of sexual activity between women makes exposure less likely than between men or between men and women.

Q: How safe are condoms?

A: Condoms are the best possible protection that we have right now. Condoms are a good way to protect yourself if you remember that they are not foolproof and that even with their use you should know with whom you're having sex in the first place.

Q: What is the most dangerous sexual activity?

A: Rectal intercourse is the most dangerous because of the increased amount of trauma possible and the possibility of blood being exchanged.

Q: Are any other sexual activities especially dangerous?

A: Anytime sexual activity is prolonged and excessively promiscuous it becomes dangerous because of the possibility of irritation, bleeding, and the exchange of blood.

Q: Can you get AIDS from casual contact such as shaking hands?

A: No. Doctors all over the country shake hands with their AIDS patients. Nurses and medical personnel in blood banks shake hands with patients, and no one has ever reported contact with the disease through this kind of casual contact.

Q: Can you get AIDS from eating in restaurants?

A: No. AIDS cannot be acquired through casual contact in any area. This is especially true in public eating places where utensils are washed regularly, because the AIDS virus is sensitive to heat and air.

Q: Can you get AIDS from swimming pools?

A: No. It is highly unlikely that you will get AIDS in a swimming pool; the AIDS virus is sensitive to chlorine, and pools are chlorinated. The same is true of swimming in lakes and oceans because the water is so hugely diluted that a single virus would die before it had a chance to invade anyone.

Q: Can you get AIDS from dirty toilet seats or bathrooms?

A: You cannot get AIDS from any kind of casual contact. There is no doubt that AIDS is transmitted primarily through sexual contact or through blood contamination.

Q: If you work in a hospital, should you take special precautions to avoid AIDS?

A: People who work in hospitals where the unexpected is likely to occur should take precautions in handling needles and other instruments that might be used to contact the blood of a patient who has been exposed or has the virus. Despite this, needle accidents are not common in hospitals, and it is extremely rare for anyone to get the disease through this kind of brief and casual contact.

Q: Should AIDS patients be quarantined?

A: AIDS patients are not dangerous to other people as long as they do not have sexual contact or allow their blood to enter another person's bloodstream. Quarantine, therefore, seems inappropriate unless a person deliberately sets out to infect other people. Such people should be dealt with on an individual basis. They are either mentally disturbed or criminally negligent and liable to prosecution.

Q: Can AIDS affect your mind?

A: AIDS is a retrovirus; that is, it can slowly affect the body, and sometimes it manifests itself with mental symptoms before anything else shows up. We are likely to see more and more people mentally deranged from AIDS as time goes on if they are persons in whom the virus attacks the brain tissue before it affects the immune system.

Q: Can you get AIDS from casual sex?

A: It is not likely that a single exposure to AIDS will result in infection. The problem is, however, that you can't be sure which time might be the exception to the rule. Generally, repeated sexual contact with an infected person will result in the disease. Single contacts are less likely to bring it about, but it is still dangerous to expose yourself in this manner.

Q: Can a man get AIDS from having sex with a prostitute?

A: Only if the prostitute is infected with AIDS in the first place. There is no way to know, and many prostitutes who have positive blood tests continue to ply their trade. The likelihood of a man getting AIDS from an infected woman is far less than of a woman getting AIDS from an infected man. In the woman the infected semen can remain in her vagina for hours or even days, waiting for an opportunity to enter her blood. The man enters and leaves the female body within a brief period and therefore is far less likely to exposure.

Q: Should you always use condoms?

A: A couple who are monogamous, have never been exposed to the virus, and have no outside exposure undergo no real risk of transmitting the disease to each other and do not need to use condoms or other protection. People who cannot be sure about the exposure of the partner are always safer when they take out the insurance policy of purchasing condoms and using them.

Q: Can you get AIDS from a blood transfusion?

A: You cannot get AIDS from donating blood. Several years ago you might have contracted AIDS from receiving blood. The likelihood of getting AIDS from a blood transfusion now is minimal, although you should never have a blood transfusion unless your doctor feels that it is essential. Every conceivable step to protect the blood supply is being taken and the likelihood of AIDS contamination is minimal.

Q: Can you get AIDS from being in a hospital in which another patients has AIDS?

A: Since AIDS is not contracted in any way except blood infection and sexual contact, you cannot get AIDS from having an AIDS patient in the same room with you unless the two of you have sexual contact or you accept some kind of blood from him. Both of these contingencies are extremely unlikely, and therefore it is quite safe to be in the same hospital with patients with AIDS.

Q: Is AIDS as dangerous as everybody says?

A: There have been no known cases of recovery of people who have contracted the disease and started to have clinical symptoms. Once the disease manifests itself, it seems to be uniformly fatal. Whether people with AIDS related complex (ARC) will develop full-blown AIDS is not yet clear. It seems likely that that will be the case. Therefore, anyone who has a positive blood test and develops symptoms probably will die.

Q: Will there ever be a cure?

A: There is no doubt that sooner or later we will overcome this disease, as we have all the others that have challenged us in the past. It may take years, but eventually the riddle will be solved.

Glossary

acronym	Word formed from the initial letters of a multiword term, as radar from *radio detecting and ranging*.
AIDS	Acronym for acquired immune deficiency syndrome.
antibody	Protein produced in the body in response to invasion by a foreign substance and having the capacity of neutralizing or reacting to that substance.
autologous	Derived from the same organism or from one of its parts, as in giving blood to yourself.
antitoxin	Substance formed in blood to act against a specific toxin or poison.
AZT	Abbreviation for the chemical name azidothymidine, an antiviral chemical shown to prolong life in some AIDS patients.
B cell	White blood cell that produces chemicals called antibodies to destroy foreign substances.
bisexual	Person, male or female, who has sexual relations with members of either sex.
diplococcus	Any one of a group of parasitic bacteria that occur in pairs, such as the germ that causes gonorrhea.
gay	Vernacular term for a homosexual.
gonococcus	The microorganism that causes gonorrhea.
gonorrhea	Venereal disease caused by the gonococcus and characterized by inflammation

	of the mucous membrane of the genitourinary tract and a discharge of mucus and pus; generally transmitted by sexual intercourse.
hemoglobin	Red pigment of the red blood corpuscles; carries oxygen from the lungs to the tissues and carbon dioxide from the tissues to the lungs.
herpes	Any of several viral infections of the skin. Herpes genitalia occurs around the skin and mucous membrane of the genital area; herpes simplex is the form of the virus that causes cold sores; herpes zoster causes the skin and nerve disease called shingles.
heterosexual	Having sexual relations with members of the opposite sex.
HIV 1	Abbreviation for human immuno-deficiency virus. This term has now been agreed upon internationally to describe the virus responsible for acquired immune deficiency syndrome. HIV 1 is the specific virus which has been isolated that causes this disease.
HIV 2	Variant of the HIV 1 virus. This has been found in some women in Africa, and appears to be a mutation from the HIV 1 virus, although basically retaining most of the essential structures of the first described virus. It appears to cause a syndrome similar to AIDS in people in Central Africa.
HTLV III	The third of the Human Type Lymphadenopathy viruses discovered in the United States. It was found to be the cause of AIDS. By international agreement, it is now called HIV 1 all over the world.

homosexual	Having sexual relations with members of the person's own sex.
immune	Not susceptible to specific disease; protected, as by inoculation.
immune body	Substance giving immunity to a specific disease, produced in the blood and lymph of persons exposed to or inoculated with the disease-causing antigen.
intercourse	Sexual joining of two persons; coitus; copulation.
interferon	Substance made by the immune system, probably in the B cells, which acts to prevent viruses from entering the cells. It is believed to act at the cell membrane, preventing the entrance of foreign particles.
interleukin	Substance produced by white blood cells and believed to destroy viral particles and germ particles by interfering with their metabolism.
LAV	Term, introduced in France, for the virus that causes acquired immune deficiency syndrome. It is an abbreviation for lymphadenopathy virus. By international agreement, it is now called HIV 1.
Lesbian	Female homosexual.
metabolism	Chemical and physical processes continuously going on in living organisms, comprising those by which food is built up into protoplasm and those by which protoplasm is used and broken down into waste matter, with the release of energy for all vital processes.
mucous membrane	A mucus-secreting membrane lining body cavities and canals that connect with the external air; as the alimentary canal, the

	respiratory tract, and the reproductive organs.
Pasteurella pestis	The specific organism that caused the Black Plague.
plague	Deadly disease that causes widespread deaths; specifically the Black Plague or bubonic plague that decimated the population of Asia and Europe in the fourteenth century.
red blood cells	(red blood corpuscles or erythrocytes) Small circular disks with both faces concave, containing hemoglobin.
spirochete	Bacterial organism; any member of the order Spirochaetales, several of which cause disease and one of which causes syphilis.
syphilis	Infectious venereal disease caused by a spirochete and usually transmitted by sexual intercourse or acquired congenitally.
T cell	Leucocyte, or white blood cell, in the immune system that identifies the chemical nature of invading organisms..
T helper cell	Leucocyte, or white blood cell, that acts to transmit the coded structure of an invading protein to B cells in order to make antibodies against the foreign organism.
trypanosome	Protozoan organism that lives as a single-cell parasite in the blood of man and other animals, often causing serious disease such as sleeping sickness.
vaccine	Preparation of dead bacteria or viruses introduced into the body to produce immunity to a specific disease by causing the formation of antibodies.
virus	Any of a group of ultramicroscopic or sub-

microscopic infectious agents that cause disease. Viruses are capable of multiplying in connection with living cells and are variously regarded as living organisms and as complex proteins.

white blood cells (leucocytes) Small colorless cells in the blood, lymph, and tissues that move about like amoebae and destroy disease-causing organisms.

Bibliography

Adams, Moody. *AIDS, You Just Think You're Safe.* Global TN, 1986.

AIDS: Ending the Fear Plague. Do It Now, 1986.

Altman, Dennis. *AIDS in the Mind of America.* Doubleday, 1986.

Antonio, Gene. *The AIDS Cover-Up? The Real and Alarming Facts about AIDS.* Ignatius Press, 1986.

Baker, Janet. AIDS. *Everything You Must Know about Acquired Immune Deficiency Syndrome.* R & E Publishers, 1983.

Black, David. *The Plague Years: A Chronicle of AIDS, Epidemic of Our Times.* Simon & Schuster, 1986.

Coping with AIDS. Department of Health & Human Services publication 85-1432. Government Printing Office, 1986.

Durham, Jerry, and Cohen, Felissa L. *The Person with AIDS: A Nursing Perspective.* Springer Publications, 1987.

Gays and Acquired Immune Deficiency Syndrome (AIDS) A Bibliography. Revisionist Press, 1986.

Ide, Arthur F. *AIDS Hysteria.* Monument Press, 1986.

Institute of Medicine and National Academy of Sciences. *Mobilizing Against AIDS: The Unfinished Story of a Virus.* Harvard University Press, 1986.

McKusick, Leon, ed. *What to Do about AIDS: Physicians and Mental Health Professionals Discuss the Issues.* University of California Press, 1986.

Martelli, Leonard J., et al. *When Someone You Love Has AIDS.* Crown, 1987.

Moffatt, Bettyclare. *When Someone You Love Has AIDS: A Book of Hope for Family and Friends.* NAL, 1987.

List of Crisis Centers

ALABAMA

MONTGOMERY

Department of Health
Room #900
State Office Building
Montgomery, AL 36130
(205) 261-5131

Jefferson County Health Department
1400 Sixth Avenue South
Birmingham, AL 35202
(205) 933-9110 Ext 441

ALASKA

ANCHORAGE

Alaska Department of Health
3601 C Street   Pouch 6333
Anchorage, AK 99502
(907) 561-4233

Anchorage S.T.D. Clinic
825 L Street

Anchorage, AK 99506
(907) 964-4611

ARIZONA

TUCSON

Metropolitan Community Church (M.C.C.)
560 South Stone Avenue
Tucson, AZ 85701
(602) 622-4536

Tucson AIDS Project
80 West Cushing Street
Tucson, AZ 85701
(602) 792-3772

PHOENIX

Arizona AIDS Fund—Trust   Mobilization Against AIDS
Lesbian and Gay Community Service Bureau/AIDS Info
5150 North 7th Street
Phoenix, AZ 85014
(602) 277-1929

Metropolitan Community Church (M.C.C.)
1029 East Turney
Phoenix, AZ 85036
(602) 265-2831

Department of Health
State Epidemiologist and AIDS Coordinator

Ramada Hall
431 North 24th Street
Phoenix, AZ 85008
(602) 255-1200

ARKANSAS

LITTLE ROCK

Gay Counseling Service
Psychotherapy Center
409 Walnut Street
Little Rock, AR 72205
(501) 663-6455 ans. serv. 24 hrs., 7 days

G.Y.S.T. House
(Get Your Stuff Together)
1616 West 14 Street
Little Rock, AR 72207
(501) 375-5151   M−F   9:00am−9:00pm

Arkansas Department of Health
4801 West Markham
Little Rock, AR
(501) 661-2395

CALIFORNIA

STATEWIDE TOLL-FREE HL—NORTHERN (800) 367-2437
   M−F 9:00am−9:00pm

S/S 11:00am–5:00pm
SOUTHERN (800) 922-2437 7 DAYS 8:00am–11pm

BERKELEY

Berkeley Gay Men's Clinic
2339 Durrant Avenue
Berkeley, CA 94704
(415) 644-0425

Social Security AIDS Community Liaison
Area Director's Office
200 Center Street Rm 308
Berkeley, CA 94704
(415) 486-3264

DUARTE

City Of Hope Medical Center
1500 East Duarte Road
Duarte, CA 91010
(818) 359-8111 ext. 2202, 2201

FRESNO

Gay United Services of Fresno
606 East Belmont
Fresno, CA 93794
(209) 264-2436

Central Valley AIDS Team
PO Box 9773
Fresno, CA 93794

HL—(209) 264-2437   Mon–Sun—10am–7pm

GARDEN GROVE

AIDS Response Program
12832 Garden Grove Boulevard
Suite E.
Garden Grove, CA 92643
(714) 534-0862

HL—(714) 534-3261   M–F   6:30pm–10:30pm/Sat & Sun
   10:30am–10:30pm

GUERNEVILLE

River Community Services   (mailing address)
15999 River Road   PO Box 312
Guerneville, CA 95446   Guerneville, CA 95446
(707) 887-2226

HL—(707) 579-AIDS   M–F   9:00am–7:00pm

OAKLAND/EASTBAY

Aids Project of the East Bay
400 40th Street Suite 200
Oakland, CA 94609
(415) 420-8181

New Life Metropolitan Community Church
685 14th Street
Oakland, CA 94612
(415) 839-4212

Alameda County Health Agency
Public Health Service
499 5th Street
Oakland, CA 94607
(415) 874-6951

LONG BEACH

AIDS Project
Long Beach Health Department
2655 Pine Avenue
Long Beach, CA 90806
(213) 427-7421 ext. 236

LOS ANGELES

American Federation for AIDS Research (AMFAR)
9601 Wilshire Blvd.
Beverly Hills, Ca 90212

AIDS Project/L.A.
7362 Santa Monica Blvd.
Los Angeles, CA 90046-6619
(213) 876-8951

HL—(213) 871-2437   M–F   9am–9pm
     (800) 922-2437   M–F   9am–9pm   Sat/Sun 10am–6pm

Computerized Aids Information Network (CAIN)
1213 North Highland Avenue   333 Valencia St. 4th Fl.
Hollywood, CA 90038   San Francisco, CA 94103
(213) 464-7400 ext. 277   (415) 864-4376

Metro Community Christian Video
5370 North Cahuenga Blvd.
North Hollywood, CA 91601

Gay and Lesbian Community Services Center
1213 North Highland Avenue
Hollywood, CA 90038
(213) 464-7276 ext. 267

L.A. Shanti Foundation
9060 Santa Monica Blvd. Suite 301
West Hollywood, CA 90069
(213) 273-7591

AID For AIDS
6985 Santa Monica Blvd
Suite 109-171
Los Angeles, CA 90046
(213) 461-6959

Southern California Physicians For Human Rights
7985 Santa Monica Boulevard
Suite 109
West Hollywood, CA 90069
(213) 464-7666

AIDS Prevention Clinic
Gay/Lesbian Community Service Center
1213 North Highland Avenue
Hollywood, CA 90038
(213) 464-7276 ext. 267   M–Th   1pm–3pm

Social Security AIDS Community Liaison
6730 Sunset Blvd.
PO Box 1391
Hollywood, CA 90078
(213) 468-3188

L.A. County U.S.C. Hospital
1200 North State Street
Los Angeles, CA 90033
(213) 226-7504

U.C.L.A. AIDS Center	(mailing address) U.C.L.A. AIDS Clinic
Wadsworth 691-W111P	U.C.L.A. Medical Center
Los Angeles, CA 90073	Los Angeles, CA 90073
(213) 206-6414	(213) 825-1251

L.A. City/County AIDS Task Force
313 North Figueroa Street
Room 924
Los Angeles, CA 90012
(213) 517-3228

L.A. City/County Public Health Department
313 North Figueroa Street
Suite 936
Los Angeles, CA 90012
(213) 974-8101   M–F   9am–5pm

U.C.L.A. Hospital
V.A. Wadsworth Medical Center

Building #500 Room 6404
Los Angeles, CA 90073
(213) 825-9412

Hemophilia Center
Orthopedic Hospital
2400 South Flower Street
Los Angeles, CA 90007
(213) 742-1358

AIDS Response Program
Gay and Lesbian Community Service Center of Orange County
12832 Garden Grove Blvd. #E
Garden Grove, CA 92643
(714) 534-0862 (10:00am–6:00pm)

Visiting Nurses   (mailing address)
1337 Braden Court   PO Box 1129
Orange, CA 92668   Orange, CA 92668
(714) 771-1209

HL—(714) 771-1209 Mon–Sun 24 hrs.

Univ. of California/Irvine Medical Center
101 City Drive South
Orange, CA 96668
(714) 634-5811

PALM SPRINGS

Desert AIDS Project
Community Counselling Center

PO Box 8925
Palm Springs, CA 92263
(619) 323-2118 (24 hour service)

SACRAMENTO

Aquarian Effort Medical Clinic
1900 K St. #103
Sacramento, CA 95814
(916) 446-6468

Sacramento AIDS Foundation
1900 K Street
#201
Sacramento, CA 98514
(916) 448-2437 M–F 9am–5pm

U.C. Davis Medical Center
2221 Stockton Boulevard
Sacramento, CA 95816
(916) 453-2004

Social Security AIDS Community Liaison
Areas Director's Office
PO Box 214008
Sacramento, CA 95821
(916) 484-4788

AIDS Project   (mailing address)
California Dept. of   AIDS Project
  Health Services   California Dept. of

1808 14th Street Suite #201   Health Services
Sacramento, CA 95814   PO Box #2230
(916) 322-2087   Sacramento, CA 95814

SAN DIEGO

San Diego AIDS Project
4304 Third Avenue   PO Box 89049
San Diego, CA 92103   San Diego, CA 92138
(619) 543-0300

Beach Area Community Clinic (Gay Male Screening Program)
3705 Mission Boulevard
San Diego, CA 92109
(619) 488-0644   Wed/Thur 6pm–9pm

San Diego County Regional Task Force on AIDS
San Diego Health Department
1700 Pacific Highway
San Diego, CA 92101
(619) 236-2705

SAN FRANCISCO

AIDS Activity Office
Room #323
101 Grove Street
San Francisco, CA 94102
(415) 558-2381

HL—(415) 863-2437   M–F   9:00am–9:00pm   Sat/Sun
      11:00am–5:00pm

AIDS Fund/San Francisco
1550 California Street
Suite 3
San Francisco, CA 94109
(415) 441-6407

AIDS Health Project
333 Valencia Street, 4th floor
San Francisco, CA 94103
(415) 626-6637

Social Security AIDS Regional Coordinator
(AZ, CA, HI, GUAM, NV)
100 Van Ness Avenue, 24th floor
San Francisco, CA 94102
(415) 556-7029

Bay Area Physicians For Human Rights
PO Box 14546
San Francisco, CA 94114
(415) 558-9353

HL—(415) 372-7321 24-hour answering machine

San Francisco AIDS Foundation
333 Valencia Street 4th floor
San Francisco, CA 94103
(415) 864-4376

HL—(415) 863-2437   M–F   9am–9pm, Sat/Sun   11am–5pm
       1-800-FOR AIDS (toll free in Northern California)

People With AIDS—S.F.
519 Castro Street #M-46
San Francisco, CA 94114

Shanti Project
890 Hayes Street
San Francisco, CA 94117
(415) 558-9644   M – F   9-5 also 24-hour answering service

Women's AIDS Network
c/o SF AIDS Foundation
333 Valencia Street 4th floor
San Francisco, CA 94103
(415) 864-4376

District Health Center II
1301 Pierce Street
San Francisco, CA 94115
(415) 558-3256

Haight Ashbury Free Medical Clinic
IV-Drug Users Program
529 Clayton
San Francisco, CA 94117
(415) 621-2014 or 621-2015

Kaposi's Sarcoma Clinic
University of California

400 Parnassus
Room A-328
San Francisco, CA 94143
(415) 66-3226

Outpatient AIDS Clinic
San Francisco General Hospital
Ward 86
995 Potrero
San Francisco, CA 94110
(415) 821-8830

In-Patient AIDS Unit
San Francisco General Hospital
Ward 5-A
1001 Potrero
San Francisco, CA 94110
(415) 821-8153

Youth Projects, Inc.-Free Medical Clinic
558 Clayton
San Francisco, CA 94117
(415) 431-2450

SAN JOSE

AIDS Project
Department of Public Health
2220 Moorpark Avenue
San Jose, CA 94128
(408) 299-5858

SANTA ANA

Special Disease Clinic
Department of Public Health
1725 West 17th Street
Santa Ana, CA 92706
(714) 834-3101

SANTA BARBARA

Tri County AIDS Task Force
300 San Antonio Road
Third Floor, Bld. B
Santa Barbara, CA 93110
(805) 967-2311

Santa Barbara Health Department
Health Care Services
300 North San Antonio Road
Santa Barbara, CA 93110
(805) 967-2311 Ext. 455

HL—(805) 963-3636   M–F   8am–5pm

WHITTIER

Area Director's Office
13215 East Penn Suite 301
Whittier, CA 90608
(714) 994-6525

COLORADO

ASPEN

Community Health Services
0100 Lonepine Road
Aspen, CO 81611
(303) 925-1185

BOULDER

University of Colorado Health Clinic
Section B - Outpatient Section
University of Colorado Health Services Center
7200 East 9th Street & Colorado Boulevard
Boulder, CO
(303) 394-8879 Mon, Wed, Fri 6:30–9:30pm

COLORADO SPRINGS

El Paso County Health Department Clinic
501 North Foote Street
Colorado Springs, CO 80909
(303) 578-3148

HL—(303) 417-4357

DENVER

Colorado AIDS Project   (mailing address)
1577 Clarkson   PO Box 18529
Denver, CO 80203   Denver, CO 80218
(303) 837-0166 Mon–Fri 9:00am–9:00pm
                24-hour answering machine

Denver Disease Control
605 Bannock
Denver, CO 80204
(303) 893-7051

National Jewish Hospital Medical Center/National Asthma
Center
3800 East Colfax Avenue
Denver, CO 80206
(303) 398-1280

Social Security AIDS Regional Coordinator
  (CO, MT, ND, SD, UT, WY)
Federal Office Building   The   Colorado   Health
1961 Stout Street, Rm 737   Network
Denver, CO 80294   P.O. Box 18529
(303) 844-3346   Denver, CO 80218
                                  (303) 837-0166

Social Security AIDS Community Liaison
1845 Sherman Way
Denver, CO 80203
(303) 844-2786

LAKEWOOD

Hospice of Saint John-Denver
1320 Everett Court
Lakewood, CO 80215
(303) 232-7900

CONNECTICUT

HARTFORD

AIDS Project Hartford
PO Box 6723
Hartford, CT 06106
(203) 247 AIDS

Epidemiology AIDS Coordinator
Connecticut Department of Health
150 Washington Street
Hartford, CT 06106
(203) 566-5058

Social Security AIDS Community Liaison
Ribicoff Federal Building
450 Main Street
PO Box 784
Hartford, CT 06120
(203) 722-3180

Hartford Gay Health Collective
281 Collins Street
Hartford, CT 06120
(203) 724-5194   Thursday 6:30–9:00pm

NEW HAVEN

AIDS Project—New Haven
PO Box 636

New Haven, CT 06503
(203) 624-0947   W-F   9-4:30

Hotline: (203) 624-2437   Mon-Fri   6:30-9:00pm

Medical Clinic
Yale-New Haven Hospital
20 York Street
New Haven, CT 06511
(203) 785-4629

Social Security AIDS Community Liaison
Giaimo Federal Building
Room 325A
150 Court Street
New Haven, CT 06510
(203) 773-2170

DELAWARE

WILMINGTON

Delaware Lesbian and Gay Health Advocates
608 West 28th Street
Wilmington, DE 19802
(302) 652-3310   M-F   10:00am-6:00pm

HL—(302) 764-2208   Mon-Sat   6:00pm-10:00pm
   answering machine

FLORIDA

24 HOUR TOLL-FREE STATE WIDE AIDS INFORMATION
1-800-352-2437

FT. LAUDERDALE

AIDS Center One
604 SW 12 Ave
Ft. Lauderdale, FL 33312
(305) 764-3123
800-325-5371 9:00–5:00   M – F   12:00–5:00 S/S

Broward County Hotline
Tuesday Night Group
c/o MCC
330 S.W. 27th St.
Ft. Lauderdale, FL 33580
(305) 537-3235 [24-hr. answering service]

FORT MYERS

Project Hope
(813) 334-4443

KEY WEST

AIDS Education Project, Inc.
513 Fleming St. Suite 14   (mailing address)
Key West, FL 33040   PO Box 4073
(305) 294-8302   9:00–5:00   Key West, FL 33041

Florida Keys Memorial Hospital Clinic
5900 Junior College Road
Key West, FL 33040
(305) 294-5537

Social Security AIDS Community Liaison
Post Office Building
Room 112
Carolyn and Simonton Streets
Key West, FL 33040
(305) 294-4914

JACKSONVILLE

AIDS Project
Duval County Health Department
515 West 6th Street Rm 14
Jacksonville, FL 32206
(904) 633-3622

M,T,W,F 8:00am–5:00pm   Th 11:30am–7:30pm

AID Jacksonville
PO Box 27061
Jacksonville, FL 32205
(904) 633-3622

MIAMI

Switchboard of Miami
35 Southwest 8th Street
Miami, FL 33130

Health Crisis Network
PO Box 521546
Miami, FL 33152
(305) 634-4780 until 9:00pm

HL—(305) 634-4636   Mon–Sun   24-hour answering service

AIDS Project-University of Miami Medical School
Department of Medicine
R-60
1611 Northwest 12th Avenue
Miami, FL 33136
(305) 549-7092   Mon–Fri   8:30am–5:00pm

Institute of Tropical Medicine
1750 Northwest 168th Street
North Miami, FL 33162
(305) 947-1722

Jackson Memorial Hospital
AIDS Center
1611 Northwest 12 Avenue
Miami, FL 33136
(305) 547-6231

ORLANDO

Orange County Health Department
PO Box 3187
Orlando, FL 32802
(305) 420-3347

TAMPA

United States Veterans Administration Hospital &
University of South Florida-College of Medicine
13000 North 30th Street
Tampa, FL 33612
(813) 974-4096 8:00am–5:00pm

Tampa AIDS Network
2904 Concordia Ave.
Tampa, FL 33629
(813) 839-5939

TALLAHASSEE

Telephone Counselling and Referral Services, Inc.
Florida AIDS Hotline
PO Box 20169
Tallahassee   FL 32316
(904) 575-8100
HL—1-800-FLA-AIDS

Department of Health and Rehabilitative Services
Florida Health Program Office
Building 1, Room 115
1317 Winewood Boulevard
Tallahassee, FL 32301
(904) 488-2905

SARASOTA

Sarasota Health Dept.
2200 Ringling Blvd.
Sarasota, FL 33578
(813) 365-2020

Sarasota AIDS Support
PO Box 15143
Sarasota, FL 34277
813-497-2437

ST. PETERSBURG

SDIA
PO Box 14316
St Petersburg, FL 33733
813-586-4297

WEST PALM BEACH

Inforum—AIDS Support Group and Information
444 Bunker Road
West Palm Beach, FL 33405-3694
305-582-HELP

Hospice of West Palm Beach County
444 Bunker Road
West Palm Beach, FL 33405-3694
(305) 582-3205

GEORGIA

ATLANTA

AID Atlanta
811 Cypress Ave NE
Atlanta, GA 30308
(404) 872-0600 after 9:00pm/answering service

HL—892-2459 24-hour answering service

Georgia Association of Physicians of Human Rights
1175 Cumberland Road, NE
Atlanta, GA 30306
(404) 876-8587

Social Security AIDS Regional Coordinator
(AL, FL, GA, KY, MS, NC, SC, TN)
101 Marietta Tower
Suite 2001
PO Box 1684
Atlanta, GA 30301
(404) 221-2475

Social Security AIDS Community Liaison
3330 Peachtree Street, NE
Atlanta, GA 30308
(404) 881-2550

COLLEGE PARK

TAPP—South Regional Center
1851 Ram Runway
College Park, GA 30337
(404) 761-2745

HAWAII

HONOLULU

Life Foundation—AIDS Service Organization
Suite 104, Ward Avenue

Honolulu, HI   96814
(808) 528-1919

Sexual Identity Center
2139 Kuhio Avenue   P.O. Box 3224
Suite 213   Honolulu, HI 96801
Honolulu, HI   96801
(808) 926-1000

HL—(808) 926-2910 24-hr. recording

Hawaii Department of Health
P.O. Box 3378
Honolulu, HI 96801
(808) 548-5986

IDAHO

BOISE

M.C.C.—BOISE
1015 East Jefferson Street
Boise, ID 83702
(208) 342-6764   M–Th   6:00pm–9:00pm

Idaho Department of Health
Bureau of Preventive Medicine
Health & Welfare Building
450 West State Street
Boise, ID 83720
(208) 334-4303

ILLINOIS

CHAMPAIGN

Gay Community AIDS Project
PO Box 713
Champaign, IL 61820
(217) 351-AIDS (answering machine 24 hours)
            (volunteer Mon–Thurs 7–10pm)

CHICAGO

1-800-AID-AIDS

Howard Brown Memorial Clinic
2676 North Halstead Street
Chicago, IL 60614
(312) 871-5777   M–F   9:00am–7:00pm

HL—(312) 871-5696 Mon–1:00pm–4:00pm,
            Tues–Thurs 7:00pm–9:30pm,
            Sun 3:00pm–5:30pm

Cook County Hospital/Scheer-Sable Clinic
1835 West Harrison Street
Chicago, IL 06612
(312) 633-7810

Jackson County Health Department
342-A North Street
Murphysboro, IL 62966
(618) 684-3143
(618) 687-HELP

Oak Forest Hospital and Nursing Home
15900 South Cicero
Oak Forest, IL 60452
(312) 687-7200   M – F   8:00am – 3:00pm

Chicago Department of Health
50 West Washington
Chicago, IL 60602
(312) 744-7573   M – F   9:00am – 4:30pm

Gay and Lesbian Liaison
Mayor's Office
Chicago City Hall
121 North LaSalle
Chicago, IL 60602

Social Security AIDS Regional Coordinator
   (IL, IN, MI, MN, OH, WI)
300 South Wacker Driver
27th Floor
Chicago, IL 60606
(312) 353-1735

Social Security AIDS Community Liaison
175 West Jackson
Room A1111
Chicago, IL 60604
(312) 353-4343

INDIANA

FT. WAYNE

Ft. Wayne AIDS Task Force
222 E. Leith
Ft. Wayne, IN 46806
(219) 456-6570

INDIANAPOLIS

Indiana AIDS Task Force
c/o Community Hospital
1500 North Ritter
Indianapolis, IN 46219
317-353-5493
HL—(317) 543-6200 ans. mach. 24 hrs., 7 days

Community Hospital
1500 North Ritter
Indianapolis, IN 46219
(317) 353-5858

Indiana State Board of Health
Chronic & Communicable Disease Control
1330 West Michigan Street
Indianapolis, IN 46206
(317) 633-8414

Justice, Inc.
1537 N. Central Ave
Indianapolis, IN 46202

IOWA

DAVENPORT

Scott County Health Department
Communicable Diseases
428 Western Avenue
Davenport, IA 52801
(319) 326-8618 by appointment

DES MOINES

Division of Disease Prevention Iowa State Department of Health
Lucas State Office Building
Des Moines, IW 50319
(515) 281-5424

Central Iowa AIDS Project
2116 Grand Ave
Des Moines, IA 50312

KANSAS

TOPEKA

VD Program Director
Department of Health and Environment
Forbes Field
Building 321
Topeka, KS 66620
(913) 862-9360 ext. 494

KENTUCKY

FRANKFORT

Department of Health Services
275 East Main Street
Frankfort, KY 40621
(502) 564-3418

LEXINGTON

Community Health Trust
507 Lake Tower #407
Lexington, KY 40502

LOUISVILLE

Specialty Clinic
834 East Broadway
Louisville, KY 40204
(502) 587-3895

Hospice of Louisville
982 Eastern Parkway
Louisville, KY 40217
(502) 636-5214

LOUISIANA

NEW ORLEANS

Foundation for Health Education
P.O. Box 51537
New Orleans, LA 70151

New Orleans AIDS Task Force
906 Bourbon Street
New Orleans, LA 70116
(504) 529-3009

HL—(504) 522-AIDS   12:00–8:00pm   M–F,   2:00–8:00pm
Sat/Sun

New Orleans Social Workers Task Force
3439 Prytania
Suite 503
New Orleans, LA 70115
(504) 899-6024

Alton Ochsner Medical Foundation and Clinic
1514 Jefferson Highway
New Orleans, LA 70121
(504) 838-3000

Tulane Medical Center
1430 Tulane Avenue
New Orleans, LA 70112
(504) 588-5905

Health Department of the City of New Orleans Clinic
320 South Claiborne St.
New Orleans, LA 70112
(504) 586-4668

HL—(504) 525-1251   M–F   8am–3:30pm

Social Security AIDS Communiy Liaison
330 North Carrollton Ave
New Orleans, LA 70119
(504) 589-4761

"Respite"
Upjohn Health Care Service
1001 Howard Avenue
New Orleans, LA 70113
(504) 524-5965

SHREVEPORT

Greater Louisiana Alliance For Dignity (GLAD)
PO Box 4523
Centenary Station
Shreveport, LA 71104
(318) 222-4523

MAINE

AUGUSTA

Director of STD Program
Bureau of Health
State House
Station 11
Augusta, ME 04333
(207) 289-3746

BANGOR

Bangor Health Department/S.T.D. Clinic
103 Texas Avenue

Bangor, ME 04401
(207) 947-0700

Central Maine Health Foundation
(207) 782-6113

Tues–Thur 7:00am–11:00pm, Sun 8:00am–11:00pm

LEWISTON

Central Maine Health Foundation
Lewiston, ME
(207) 775-1267

PORTLAND

The AIDS Project
PO Box 10723
Portland, ME 04104
(207) 775-1267
1-800-851-AIDS M,W,F, 6:00–9:00pm

Telemed-1-800-442-6385

Maine Health Foundation, Inc.
PO Box 7329 DTS
Portland, ME 04112

YARMOUTH

Maine Lesbian & Gay Political Alliance
Yarmouth, ME
(207) 775-1267

MARYLAND

Statewide Hotline: 1-800-638-6252

BALTIMORE

Baltimore Hotline: 945-AIDS

Health Education and Resource Organization
(H.E.R.O)
101 West Road Suite 819
Baltimore, MD 21201
(301) 945-2437

AIDS Project of the Cancer Center
University of Maryland
22 South Green Street
Baltimore, MD 21201
(301) 528-7394

Gay/Lesbian Community Center
241 W. Changes St, 3rd Floor
Baltimore, MD
(301) 837-2050

Johns Hopkins Hospital
Blalock III
600 North Wolfe
Baltimore, MD 21205
(301) 955-3150
(301) 955-7090 Clinic

Maryland Department of Health and Mental Hygiene
Office of Disease Control
201 West Preston Street
Baltimore, MD 21201
(301) 383-2644

Social Security AIDS Community Liaison
709 Lombard Street
Baltimore, MD 21202
(301) 962-0735

BETHESDA

NIH Clinical Center
National Institute of Allergy and Infectious Disease
Bldg. 10 Room 11-B13
Bethesda, MD 20205

MASSACHUSETTS

Statewide Hotline: 1-800-235-2331

BOSTON

Social Security AIDS Regional Coordinator
  (CT, ME, MA, NH, RI, VT)
PO Box 9227
Boston, MA 02114
(617) 223-4551

Social Security AIDS Community Liaison
Park Square Building, Rm 250
31 St James Avenue
Boston, MA 02116
(617) 223-4337

Fenway Community Health Center
661 Boylston Street
Boston, MA 02116
(617) 267-7573

HL—(617) 536-7733　M–F　10:00am–8:00pm;
　　　　　　　　　　　Sat 10:00–4:00pm; Sun 12:00–4:00pm
　　　　　　　　　　　Eves & Wknds—Answering service

Beth Israel Hospital
330 Brookline Avenue
Boston, MA 02215
(617) 735-2000

Boston City Hospital
HOB 320
818 Harrison Street
Boston, MA 02118
(617) 424-5000

Massachusetts General Hospital
c/o Infectious Disease Clinic
Fruit Street
Boston, MA 02114
(617) 726-3812
(617) 726 2000 (switchboard)

New England Deaconist Hospital
185 Pilgrim Road
Boston, MA 02115
(616) 732-7000

State Task Force On AIDS
Department of Public Health
150 Tremont Street
Boston, MA 02111
(617) 727-2700

Boston City AIDS Coordinator
H.O.B. #324
818 Harrison Avenue
Boston, MA 02118
(617) 424-4744

SOMERVILLE

Omega
A Division of Catholic Charities
270 Washington Street
Sommerville, MA 02143
(617) 776-6369

SPRINGFIELD

Bay State Medical Center
759 Chestnut Street
Springfield, MA 01199
(413) 787-2500

WESTFIELD

Western Massachusetts State Hospital Hospice
91 East Mountain Road
Westfield, MA 01084
(413) 562-4131

MICHIGAN

DETROIT·

Henry Ford Hospital
2799 Grand Boulevard West
Detroit, MI 48202
(313) 876-2563

Social Security AIDS Community Liaison
McNamara Building, Rm 1000
477 Michigan Av
Detroit, MI 48226
(313) 226-3116

ROYAL OAK

Wellness Networks, Inc.
PO Box 1046
Royal Oak, MI 48068
(313) 876-3582

HL—(800) 482-2404 ext. 3582 Mon–Sat 24 hours (IN STATE)
        (800) 521-7946 ext. 3582 " "   " "
            (OUT OF STATE)

MINNESOTA

Statewide Hotline: 1-800-752-4201

MINNEAPOLIS

Minnesota AIDS Project
2025 Nicollet, Suite 200
Minneapolis, MN 55403
(612) 870-7773

Social Security AIDS Community Liaison
1811 Chicago Ave
Minneapolis, MN 55404
(612) 725-2717

MISSISSIPPI

JACKSON

Mississippi Gay Alliance
P.O. Box 8342
Jackson, MI 39204
(601) 353-7611

HL—(601) 353-7611 staffed 24 hrs, 7 days

Mississippi Department of Health
P.O. Box 1700
Jackson, MI 39201
(205) 261-5131

MISSOURI

KANSAS CITY

Gay and Lesbian Health Clinic
PO Box 2696
Kansas City, MO 64142
(816) 931-4470   M–F   5:30pm–8:00pm

Good Samaritan Project
C/O MCCKC
PO Box 10087
Kansas City, MO 64111
(816) 452-225 (24 hours)

St. Luke's Hospital
Wornall Road at 44th Street
Kansas City, MO 64111
(816) 932-2000

St. Mary's Hospital/Hospice
101 Memorial Drive
Kansas City, MO 64108
(816) 753-5700

Truman Medical Center
2301 Holmes
Kansas City, MO 64108
(816) 556-3000

Westport Free Clinic
4008 Baltimore
Kansas City, MO 64111
(816) 931-3236

Social Security AIDS Regional Coordinator (IA, KS, MO, NE)
Federal Office Building, Rm 436
601 East 12 Street
Kansas City, MO 64106
(816) 374-6195

ST. LOUIS

Metropolitan St. Louis Task Force on AIDS
PO Box 2905
St. Louis, MO 63130
(314) 658-1025

St. Louis Effort for AIDS
(314) 421-2437
HL—(314) 421-AIDS

Deaconess Hospital
6150 Oakland Avenue
St. Louis, MO 63139
(314) 645-8510

Jewish Hospital
216 South King's Highway
St. Louis, MO 63110
(314) 454-7000

St. Mary's Health Center
6420 Clayton Road
St. Louis, MO 63117
(314) 768-8000

Washington University Medical Center
Barnes Hospital Plaza
St. Louis, MO 63110
(314) 362-7135

MONTANA

Confidential Testing-Community Health Centers

Billings - 256-6821
Bozeman- 587-4297
Butte - 723-3271

Great Falls- 761-1190
Helena - 442-0121
Kalispell - 755-5300 ext.
343

HELENA

Department of Health
Cogswell Building
Helena, MT 59620
(406) 444-4740

MISSOULA

Missoula City Health
(406) 721-5700 ext. 358

NEBRASKA

LINCOLN

Office of Disease Control
State Department of Health
PO Box 95007

Lincoln, NE 68509
(402) 471-2937

NEVADA

CARSON CITY

Nevada Division of Human Services
Communicable Disease Office
505 East King Street Room 200
Carson City, NV
(702) 885-4800

LAS VEGAS

Metropolitan Community Church (MCC)
1119 South Main
Las Vegas, NV 89104
(702) 384-2325

Clark County Health District
625 Shadow Lane
Las Vegas, NV 89106
(702) 385-1291

RENO

Washoe County Health District
Nine and Wells
Reno, NV 89502
(702) 785-4290

NEW HAMPSHIRE

CONCORD

VD Program Public Health Advisor
Bureau of Communicable Disease Control
Public Health Service
Health and Welfare Building
Hazen Drive
Concord, NH 03301
(603) 271-4490

HL—(800) 852-3345   M−F   6:00pm−11:00pm

NEW JERSEY

HIGHLAND PARK

Hyacinth Foundation/New Jersey AIDS Project
308 Raritan Ave
Highland Park, NJ 08904
(201) 246-8439   9:00am−8:00pm   M−F   24-hour coverage

NEW BRUNSWICK

N.J. Lesbian and Gay AIDS Awareness
St. Michael's Medical Center
268 High Street   Box 1431
Newark, NJ 07102   New Brunswick, NJ 08930
(201) 596-0767   M−F   9:00am−5:00pm

HL—(201) 877-5525 Evenings till 11pm 7 days/week

NEWARK

AIDS Health Center
Newark Beth Israel Center
201 Lyons Ave
Newark, NJ 07112
(201) 962-8025

St. Michaels Hospital
306 Martin Luther King Blvd.
Newark, NJ 07102
(201) 877-5525

HL—(201) 596-0767   M–F   evenings

Social Security AIDS Community Liaison
970 Broad Street Rm 1035
Newark, NJ 07102
(201) 645-3247

University Hospital
100 Bergen Street
Newark, NJ 07103
(201) 456-6000

TRENTON

St. Francis Hospital
601 Hamil
Trenton, NJ 08629

(609) 599-5000
Mid-state Prison (609) 723-4221 ext. 228

NEW MEXICO

New Mexico AIDS Task Force
Department of Health and Environment
State of New Mexico
209A McKenzie
Santa Fe, NM 87501

HL—(505) 984-0911   M–F   9:00am–5:00pm

New Mexico AIDS Servces, Inc.
209A McKenzie Street
Sante Fe, NM 87501
(505) 984-0911   M–F   1:00pm–5:00pm

HL—1-800-858-AIDS daily 7:00pm–10:00pm

NEW YORK

STATEWIDE TOLL-FREE HOTLINE (800) 462-1884 7 DAYS
8AM-MIDNIGHT

ALBANY

AIDS Council of Northeastern New York
332 Hamilton Street
Albany, NY 12210
(518) 434-4686

HL—(518) 445-2437 7 days 7pm–9pm (24-hr. answering machine)

Albany Medical Center
New Scotland Avenue
Albany, NY 12208
(518) 445-3125

New York State AIDS Institute
New York State Department of Health
Albany, NY 12237
(518) 473-0641

HL—(800) 462-1884

BINGHAMTON

Binghamton AIDS Task Force Southern Tier 56 Whitney Avenue Binghamton, NY 13901 (607) 772-2803 9:00–5:00	(mailing address) Broome County Health Dept. 1 Wall Street Binghamton, NY 13901

HL—(607) 723–6520 M–F 7pm–9pm

BUFFALO

Western New York AIDS Program
PO Box 38, Bidwell Station

Buffalo, NY 14222
(716) 881-2437

HL—(716) 881-2347

NEWBURGH

St. Luke's Hospital
70 DuBois Street
PO Box 631
Newburgh, NY 12550
(914) 561-4400

NEW YORK CITY

American Foundation For AIDS Research
40 West 57th Street
Suite 406
New York, NY 10019
(212) 333-3118

AIDS Resource Center   (mailing address)
152 8th Ave   PO Box 792, Chelsea Station
New York, NY 10011   New York, NY 10011
(212) 206-1414

American Red Cross Transportation & Home Attendant Pgm.
150 Amsterdam Ave.
New York, NY 10023
(212) 787-1000 exts. 8200, 8202

Hours: M-F: 9am–4pm

Citizens United For Research and Education for AIDS
1726 Stuyvesant Station
New York, NY 10009
212-243-9010

Gay Men's Health Crisis, Inc.
254 West 18th Street
New York, NY
(212) 807-7035

(mailing address)
P.O. Box 274
132 West 24th St.
New York, NY 10011

HL—(212) 807-6655 M–F 10:30am–9pm (Service other hours)

Haitian Coalition on AIDS
255 Eastern Parkway
Brooklyn, NY 11238
(718) 735-3568

HL—(718) 855-0972 M–F 9am–5pm

H.E.A.L. [formerly Wipe Out Aids]
227 Waverly Place
New York, NY

People With AIDS
Box G-27
444 Hudson Street
New York, NY 10014
(212) 242-0545 7 DAYS (answering machine)

PWA Coalition Newsline
PO Box 197
Murray Hill Station
New York, NY 10156
(212) 242-3900 (service)

Hispanic AIDS Forum
Medical Contact: (212) 477-8866

Albert Einstein College of Medicine
Pediatric AIDS Hotline
(212) 430-3333

Bellevue Hospital
New York University Medical Center
First Avenue & 27th Street
New York, NY 10016
(212) 561-5151

Beth Israel Medical Center
10 Nathan Place
New York, NY 10003
(212) 420-2650

Cabrini Medical Center
227 East 19th Street
New York, NY 10003
(212) 725-6000

Columbia Presbyterian Medical Center
622 West 168th Street
New York, NY 10032
(212) 694-2500

Cornell University Medical Center
1300 York Avenue
New York, NY 10021
(212) 472-5454

Interfaith Medical Center
555 Prospect Place
Brooklyn, NY 11238
(718) 240-1767

Long Island College Hospital
Family Care Center
(718) 780-1855

Mount Sinai Medical Center
Madison Avenue at 99th Street
New York, NY 10029
(212) 650-6500

Roosevelt Hospital and AIDS Clinic
St. Luke's–Roosevelt Hospital Center
428 West 59th Street
New York, NY 10019
(212) 554-7221

St. Luke's Hospital
421 West 113th Street
New York, NY 10025
(212) 870-6000

Memorial/Sloan-Kettering Hospital
1275 York Avenue
New York, NY 10021
(212) 794-7722

AIDS Unit
New York City Human Rights Commission
52 Duane Street
New York, NY 10007
(212) 566-1826 or 566-5446

Office of Gay and Lesbian Health Concerns
New York City Department of Health
125 Worth Street   Box 67
New York, NY 10013   New York, NY 10013
(212) 566-4995

Social Security AIDS Regional Coordinator (NY, NJ, PR, VI)
26 Federal Plaza, Rm 743
New York, NY 10278
(212) 264-7299

PATCHOGUE

Social Security AIDS Community Liaison
75 Oak Street
Patchogue, NY 11772
(516) 475-6996

PLATTSBURGH

Champlain Valley Physicians Hospital
CVPH Medical
100 Beekman Street
Plattsburgh, NY 12901
(518) 561-2000

ROCHESTER

AIDS-Rochester/Rochester AIDS Task Force
153 Liberty Pole Way
Rochester, NY 14604
(716) 232-7181   M—F   9:30am—4:30pm

HL—(716) 244-8640   M—F   24 hr.

University Health & Services
University of Rochester   Strong Memorial Hospital
250 Crittenden Blvd.   601 Elmwood Avenue
Rochester, NY 14620   Rochester, NY 14642
(716) 275-5871

Social Security AIDS Community Liaison
100 State Street
Room 500
Rochester, NY 14614
(716) 263-6814

STONYBROOK

Long Island AIDS Project
LIAP—SAHP—HSC
SUNY At Stonybrook
Stonybrook, NY 11794
(516) 444-2437

SYRACUSE

AIDS Task Force of Central New York
Room 407   (mailing address)
306 S. Salina Street   PO Box 1911
Syracuse, NY 13202   Syracuse, NY 13201
(315) 475-2430

HL—(315) 475-2437   M–F   7:30pm–9:30pm

OMAHA

Nebraska AIDS Project, Inc.
PO Box 3512
Omaha, NE 68103
(402) 345-5637 or 341-9448

HL—800-782-AIDS   (statewide   except   Omaha—342-4233)
    6:00pm–11:00pm daily

NORTH CAROLINA

CHARLOTTE

Metrolina AIDS Project
PO Box 32662
Charlotte, NC 28232
(704) 333-2437 9:00am–6:00pm with machine
              6:00pm–9:00pm M–F

DURHAM

U.S. Veterans Administration Hospital
508 Fulton Street

Durham, NC 27705
(919) 286-0411

Lesbian and Gay Health Project
P.O. Box 3203
Durham, NC 27705
(919) 286-0079
Mon–Fri 7pm–9pm 24-hour answering machine

Durham County Health Services
224 Main Street
Durham, NC
(919) 688-8176

PITTSBORO

East Chatham Medical Center
Route 7 Box 7
Pittsboro, NC 27312
(919) 542-2731

NORTH DAKOTA

BISMARCK

Division of Disease Control
Department of Health
State Capitol
Bismarck, ND 58505
(701) 224-2378

OHIO

STATEWIDE   TOLL-FREE   HL   (800)   322-2437
M–F   4:00pm–11:00pm S/S 7:00pm–11:00pm

AIDS Advisory Committee
Ohio Dept. of Health
246 N. High Street
Columbus,OH 43216
(614) 466-4643

AKRON

Akron City AIDS Task Force
Akron Health Department
177 South Broadway
Akron, OH 44308
(216) 375-2960

Children's Hospital Medical Center
281 Locust Street
Akron, OH 44308
(216) 379-8200

CANTON

Canton City AIDS Task Force
Canton City Health Department
City Hall
Canton, OH 44702
(216) 489-3231

CINCINNATI

AIDS Volunteers of Cincinnati
P.O. Box #19009
Cincinnati, OH 45219
(513) 421-7585

Cincinnati AIDS Task Force
U.C. College of Medicine
231 Bethesda Avenue
Cincinnati, OH 45267
(513) 352-3143

HL—(513) 352-3138   M–F   9:00am–6:00pm

Social Security AIDS Community Liaison
Federal Building, Rm 2008
550 Main Street
Cincinnati, OH 45202
(513) 684-2685

Ambrose Clenent Health Clinic
3101 Burnet Avenue
Cincinnati, OH 45229
(513) 730-4300 7:30am–4:20pm

Children's Hospital Medical Center
Elland and Bethesda Avenues
Cincinnati, OH 45221

CLEVELAND

Cleveland/Cuyahoga AIDS Task Force
Cleveland Health Dept.
1925 South Clair Avenue
Cleveland, OH 44114
(216) 664-2525

Gay Education and Awareness Resources
2100 Fulton Road   P.O. Box #6177
Cleveland, OH 44102   Cleveland, OH 44101
(216) 651-1999

HL—(800) 332-2437   M–S   4:00pm–11:00pm

Health Issues Task Force
PO Box 14925-Public Square
Cleveland, OH 44114
(216) 651-1448   M–F   6:00pm–11:00pm

Social Security AIDS Community Liaison
AJC Federal Building, Rm 793
1240 East 9 Street
Cleveland, OH 44199
(216) 522-4157

Cleveland Clinic Foundation
9500 Euclid Avenue
Cleveland, OH 44106
(216) 444-5258

University Hospital of Cleveland
2101 Adelbert Road

Cleveland, OH 44106
(216) 362-2069

University Hospital AIDS Referral Center
2065 Adelbert Road
Cleveland, OH 44106
(216) 844-3227

COLUMBUS

Columbus AIDS Task Force
PO Box 8393
Columbus, OH 43201
(614) 297-0411

Columbus Children's Hospital
700 Children's Drive
Columbus, OH 43205
(614) 461-2310, (614) 461-2060

Ohio State University Hospital
410 West Tenth Avenue
Columbus, OH 43210
(614) 421-8729

Ohio Department of Health
246 North High Street
Columbus, OH 43216
(614) 466-0265

STATEWIDE TOLL-FREE AIDS HOTLINE—HL—(800)
   322-2437
M–F   4:00pm–11:00pm   Sat/Sun   7:00pm–11:00pm

RAVENNA

Portage County Health Department
449 South Meridian Street
Ravenna, OH 44266
(216) 296-9919

SANDUSKY

Sandusky AIDS Task Force
Erie County Health Department
420 Superior Street   PO Box 375
Sandusky, OH 44870   Sandusky, OH 44870

TOLEDO

The Toledo Hospital
Northwest Ohio Hemophilia Center
2142 North Cove Blvd.
Toledo, OH 43606
(419) 471-5609
       471-4359

YOUNGSTOWN

Youngstown AIDS Task Force
Youngstown Health Department
City Hall, 7th floor
Youngstown, OH 44503
(216) 746-1892

Youngstown Hospital Association
Gypsy Land and Goleta Avenue
Youngstown, OH 44501
(216) 744-5558

Portland, OR 97204
(503) 223-5907   10:00am–3:00pm

Cascade AIDS Network
408 SW 2nd Ave Rm 420
Portland, OR 97204

HL—(503) 223-5907   9:00am–6:00pm   M–F

Oregon AIDS Task Force
105 35 NE Glisan
Portland, OR 97220
(503) 254-8812

HL—(503) 223-8299   10:00am–3:00pm

Oregon State Health Division
1400 SW Fifth Ave   PO Box 231
Portland, OR 97201   Portland, OR 97207
(503) 229-5792   M–F   9:00am–5:00pm

MEDFORD

People For People With AIDS
PO Box 1448
Medford, OR 97501

PENNSYLVANIA

STATEWIDE   TOLL-FREE   HL—(800) 692-7254   M–F
   7:00pm–11:00pm

DANVILLE

Geisinger Medical Center
Department of Infectious Disease
13–43
Danville, PA 17822
(717) 271-6000

HARRISBURG

State AIDS Task Force
Pennsylvania Department of Health
Health and Welfare Blvd.
Harrisburg, PA
(717) 787-3350

STATEWIDE   TOLL-FREE   HL—(800) 692-7254   M–F
    7:00pm–11:00pm

PHILADELPHIA

Philadelphia AIDS Task Force
1231 St. James Street   PO Box 7259
Philadelphia, PA 19107   Philadelphia, PA 19101
(215) 545-8686

HL—(215) 732-AIDS   11:00am–11:00pm   M–F;
    7:00pm–11:00pm S/S
    Screening and Testing (215) 735-1911

Hospice Program of Pennsylvania Hospital
8th and Spruce Streets
Philadelphia, PA 19107
(215) 829-5335

Social Security AIDS Regional Coordinator
(DE, DC, MD, PA, VA, WV)
PO Box 8788
Philadelphia, PA 19101
(215) 596-1515

PITTSBURGH

Pittsburgh AIDS Task Force
(412) 471-0101

MCC-Pittsburgh
4401 5th Avenue
Oakland, PA 15217
(412) 681-0765

Social Security AIDS Community Liaison
6117 Penn Circle North
Pittsburgh, PA 15206
(412) 361-5707

Persad, Inc.
817 Highland Building
121 South Highland Ave
Pittsburgh, PA 15206
(412) 441-0857 9:00am–5:00pm (hrs. by appt.)

Graduate School of Public Health
University of Pittsburgh
A-417 Crabtree Hall
Pittsburgh, PA 15261
(412) 624-3928

Pittsburgh Community Health Services
121 South Highland Ave
2nd floor-Highland Bldg.
Pittsburgh, PA 15206
(412) 624-5046

The Pitt Men's Research Study
P.O. Box #7319
Pittsburgh, PA 15213
(412) 624-5046

UPPER DARBY

Social Security AIDS Community Liaison
6801 Ludlow Street
Second Floor
Upper Darby, PA 19082
(215) 352-5514

PUERTO RICO

SANTURCE

Puerto Rico AIDS
Fundacion AIDS de Puerto Rico, Inc.
Avenida Ponce de Leon 1556   Call Box 8347
Oficina 3-B   Fernandez Juncos Sta.
Santurce, PR 00909   Santurce, PR 00910
HL—723-7819

RHODE ISLAND

PROVIDENCE

Rhode Island Department of Health
Division of Disease Control

75 Davis Street
Providence, RI 02908
(401) 277-2362

Rhode Island Hospital
593 Eddy Street
Providence, RI 02902
(401) 277-4000

SOUTH CAROLINA

COLUMBIA

State Department of Health and Environmental Control
Bureau of Communicable Diseases
2600 Bull Street
Columbia, SC 29201
(803) 758-5621

SOUTH DAKOTA

PIERRE

Department of Health
523 East Capitol
Pierre, SD 57501
(605) 773-3364

TENNESSEE

MEMPHIS

St. Jude's Children's Hospital
PO Box 318

Memphis, TN 38101
(901) 522-0300

University of Tennessee Center for Health Science
956 Court Ave Room 3B09
Coleman Building
Memphis, TN 38163
(901) 528-5932

NASHVILLE

Lifestyle Health Services
1727 Church Street
Nashville, TN 37203
(615) 329-1478   Tues–Thurs   5:30pm–9:00pm Sun afternoons

Nashvile C.A.R.E.S.
PO Box 25107
Nashville, TN 37202

TEXAS

AUSTIN

Austin AIDS Project
Warterloo Counseling Center
6901 N. Lamar St. Suite 111
Austin, TX 78752
(512) 452-5966

HL—(512)-452-9550

DALLAS

AIDS Resource Center
3920 Cedar Springs   PO Box 190712
Dallas, TX 75219   Dallas, Tx 75219
(214) 528-4233 or 521-5124

AIDS Project
Oak Lawn Counseling Center
5811 Nash
Dallas, TX 75235
(214) 351-1502

HL—(214) 351-4335   Mon–Sat noon–8:00pm

Parkland Hospital
5201 Perry Hines Blvd.
Dallas, TX 75235
(214) 637-8000

Baylor University Hospital
3500 Gaston Ave
Dallas, TX 75246
(214) 820-0111

Social Security AIDS Regional Coordinator
(AR, LA, NM, OK, TX)
1200 Main Tower, Rm 2100
Dallas, TX 75202
(214) 767-4281

Social Security AIDS Community Liaison
PO Box 31430
Dallas, TX 75231
(214) 767-0137

HOUSTON

Social Security AIDS Community Liaison
3910 Kirby Drive
Houston, TX 77098
. (713) 229-3451

KS/AIDS Foundation of Houston
3400, Montrose, Suite 700   PO Box 66973 Suite 1155
Houston, TX 77006   Houston, TX 77006
HL—(713) 524–2437   M-F   9:00am–9:00pm

Memorial City Hospital
920 Frostwood
Houston, TX 77024
(713) 932-3000

Methodist Hospital
6565 Fannin
Mail Stat. 910
Houston, TX 77030
(713) 790-3311

The Montrose Clinic
803 Hawthorne
Houston, TX 77006
(713) 227-6565

The Montrose Counseling Center
900 Lovett #203
Houston, TX 70076
(713) 529-0037

University of Texas Systan Cancer Center
M.D. Anderson Hospital and Tumor Institute
Texas Medical Center
Houston, TX 77030
(713) 792-2666/3020

6723 Bertner
PO Box 189
Houston, TX 77030

Houston Health Department
Park Plaza Hospital
1313 Herman Drive
Houston, TX
(713) 527-5037

Mayor's Task Force on AIDS
City of Houston
P.O. Box #1562
Houston, TX 77251
(713) 342-0100 ext. 117

SAN ANTONIO

Safeweek AIDS Project
1627 West Rosewood
Box 5481
San Antonio, TX 78201

HL—(517) 733-7300   7:00pm–11:00pm

Social Security AIDS Community Liaison
PO Box 21068
San Antonio, TX 78221
(512) 229-5662

UTAH

SALT LAKE CITY

AIDS Project/Utah
422 South 1200 E. #7
Salt Lake City, UT 84102
(801) 582-4378

Utah Community Services Center and Clinic
442 Easte 800 South
Salt Lake City, UT 84111
(801) 532-6040

HL—(801) 533-0927 seven days, 24 hrs.

Utah State Health Department
P.O. Box 45500
Salt Lake City, UT 84145
(801) 533-6191

City/County Health Department
Room #116
610 South Second Street
Salt Lake City, UT 84140
(801) 530-7500

VERMONT

BURLINGTON

Medical Center of Vermont
Given Building C-242
University of Vermont
Burlington, VT 05401
(802) 656-2345

Vermont Department of Health
60 Main Street   P.O. Box 70
Burlington, VT 05401   Burlington, VT 05401
(802) 863-7240

VIRGINIA

Toll-Free AIDS Hotline: 1-800-533-4148 (M–F: 9am–5pm)

RICHMOND

Virginia Department of Health
101 Governor Street Room 701
Richmond, VA 23219
(804) 786-6029

Toll-Free AIDS Hotline: 1-800-533-4148 (M–F: 9am-5pm)

Richmond AIDS Information Network
Fan Free Clinic
1721 Hanover Avenue
Richmond, VA 23220
(804) 355-4428   M–F   10:00am–10:00pm

HL—(804) 358-6343   M–F   2:00pm–10:00pm

NORFOLK

Tidewater AIS Task Force
814 West 44th
Norfolk, VA 23508
(804) 923-5859 9:00am–5:00pm M–F 7:00pm–9:00pm 7
days

WASHINGTON (see separate listing for *Washington D.C.*)

SEATTLE

AIDS Spiritual AID
P.O. Box 12216
Seattle, WA 98112
(206) 325-2421

AIDS Support Group
PO Box 21591
Seattle, WA 98101
(206) 322-AIDS 24-hr. messages

Hours: M–F: 1–5pm

Chicken Soup Brigade   (mailing address)
801 East Harrison   PO Box 20066
Seattle, WA 98102   Seattle, WA 98102
(206) 322-2873   M–F   8:30am–7:00pm

Community Home Health Care
190 Queen Anne N.

Seattle, WA 98109
(206) 285-7030   (24 hrs.)

Hours: M–Sun: 8am–5pm

Gay Men's Health Group
PO Box 1768
Seattle, WA 98111
(206) 322-7043

Harbor Medical Center AIDS Clinic
3rd Floor, South Wing
Harborview Medical Center
325 Ninth Ave.
Seattle, WA 98104
(206) 223-8780

Northwest AIDS Foundation
PO Box 3449
Seattle, WA 98114
(206) 587-0306

Seattle Counseling Services For Sexual Minorities
1505 Broadway
Seattle, WA 98122
(206) 329-8737   M–F   10:00am–10:00pm

Shanti-Seattle
PO Box 20698
Seattle, WA 98102
(206) 322-0279 or 324-7920 for information

Hospice of Seattle/Providence Hospital
500 17 Avenue & Greenwood Avenue North
Seattle, WA 98112
(206) 326-5398

Seattle/King's County Health Department
Seattle AIDS Assessment Clinic
1406 Public Safety Blvd.
610 Third Avenue
Seattle, WA 98104

HL—(206) 587-4999

Social Security AIDS Regional Coordinator (AK, ID, R, WA)
2901 Third Ave
Mail Stop 301
Seattle, WA 98121
(206) 442-4526

Visiting Nurse Association
811 1st Ave.
Seattle, WA 98104
(206) 382-9700 (24 hrs. on-call)

Hours: M—Sun: 8am—4:30pm

Seattle AIDS Action Committee
113 Summit Ave, East 204
Seattle, WA
(206) 323-1229 for health referrals and info.

WEST VIRGINIA

CHARLESTON

Preventive Health Services
State Department of Health
151 Eleventh Avenue
South Charleston, WV 25303

WISCONSIN

GREEN BAY

Center Project, Inc.
PO Box 1062
Green Bay, WI 54303
(414) 437-7400

KENOSHA, GREEN BAY, APPLETON, FOX VALLEY

Kenosha Hospice Alliance
625 57 Street
Suite 600
Kenosha, WI 53142
(414) 658-8344

MADISON

Madison AIDS Support Network
PO Box 731
Madison, WI 53701
(608) 255-1711

Governor's Council On Gay and Lesbian Issues
State Capitol   PO Box 7863
Madison, WI 53707   Madison, WI 53707
(608) 266-1212

Public Health Task Force on AIDS
Bureau of Community Health and Prevention
PO Box 309
Madison, WI 53701-0309
(608) 267-3583

MILWAUKEE

AIDS Resource Center of Wisconsin
PO Box 92505
Milwaukee, WI 53202
(414) 273-2437

The Milwaukee AID Project (MAP)
PO Box 92505
Milwaukee, WI 53202
(414) 273-AIDS

HL—1-800-334-AIDS (9:00am–9:00pm   M–F)

Brady East Sexually Transmitted Disease (B.E.S.T.) Clinic
1240 East Brady Street
Milwaukee, WI 53201
(414) 272-2144 Tues 7:00pm–10:pm Sat 1:00–3:00pm
               Mon 7:00pm–9:00pm Hepatitis B, HTLV-3
               Ab testing

HL—(414) 273-2437   M–F   6:00am–10:00pm

Milwaukee AIDS Project (MAP)
PO Box 92505
Milwaukee, WI 53202
(414) 273-AIDS

Cream City Association Foundation
PO Box 93002
Milwauke, WI 53202
(414) 264-3177

Milwaukee County General Hospital
87000 West Wisconsin Avenue
Milwaukee, WI 53226
(414) 257-7900

Milwaukee Hospice Home Care
1022 North 9 Street
Milwaukee, WI 53233
(414) 271-3686

Mount Sinai Hospice
6925 North Fort Washington
Glendale, WI 53217
(414) 352-3300

Saint Joseph's Hospice
5000 West Chambers
Milwaukee, WI 53210
(414) 447-2629

Saint Mary's Hospice
2320 North Lake Drive
Milwaukee, WI 53211
(414) 225-8025

Visiting Nurses Association
1540 North Jefferson
Milwaukee, WI 53202
(414) 276-2295

WYOMING

CHEYENNE

Wyoming Department of Health
Hathaway Building, 4th Floor
Cheyenne, WY 82002
(307) 777-7953

WASHINGTON, D.C.

Social Security AIDS Community Liaison
2100 M Street
PO Box 19383
Washington, DC 20036
(202) 653-7990

D.C. AIDS Task Force
Whitman Walker Clinic AIDS Program
2335 18th Street NW
Washington, D.C. 20009
(202) 332-5939

HL—(202) 332-2437   M–F   10:00am–10:00pm

George Washington University Hospital
901 23rd Street NW
Washington, D.C. 20037
(202) 676-6000

Washington Hospital Center
Section of Inf. Disease Room 2A-70
110 Irving Street NW
Washington, D.C. 20010
(202) 541-0500

Social Work HTLV-II/AIDS Clearinghouse
Social Work Services
Walter Reed Army Medical Center
Washington, DC 20307-5001
(202) 576-1378

NATIONAL ORGANIZATIONS

Non-Profit Agencies:
National Gay and Lesbian Task Force
1517 U St. N.W.
Washington DC 20009
(202) 332-6483

The Fund for Human Dignity
666 Broadway
New York, NY 10012
(212) 529-1600

HL—(800) 221-7044   M–F   3:00pm–9:00pm
    (212) 529-1604 (NY, AK, HI)

Lambda Legal Defense & Education Fund
132 West 43rd Street
New York, NY 10036
(212) 944-9488

National Gay Rights Advocates
540 Castro Street
San Francisco, CA 94114
(415) 863-3624

Gay Rights National Lobby   Mailing Address:
750 Seventh Street, S.E.   P.O. Box 1892
Washington, DC 20013   Washington, DC 20013
(202) 546-1801

National Coalition of Gay Sexually Transmitted Disease Services
PO Box 239
Milwaukee, WI 53201
(414) 277-7671

American Association of Physicians for Human Rights
P.O. Box 14366
San Francisco, CA 94114
(415) 558-9353

American Hospital Association
840 North Lake Shore Drive
Chicago, IL 60611
(312) 280-6000

AIDS Action Council of the Federation of AIDS-Related
  Organizations
1115 1/2 Independence Avenue, S.E.
Washington, D.C. 20003
(202) 547-3101

National Lesbian and Gay Health Foundation
P.O. Box 65472
Washington, D.C. 20035

National Hemophilia Association
19 West 34th Street, Suite 1204
New York, NY 10001
(212) 563-0211

HL—682-5510, Mon–Fri   9am–5pm

National Coalition of Gay Sexually Transmitted Disease Services
PO Box 239
Milwaukee, WI 53201
(414) 277-7671

FEDERAL AGENCIES:

U.S. Department of Health and Human Services
200 Independence Avenue, S.W.
Washington, D.C. 20201
(202) 245-6296

Public Health Service
Hubert H. Humphrey Bldg.
Washington, D.C. 21235

Centers For Disease Control (CDC)
AIDS Activity
Building 6, Room 292
1600 Clifton Road
Atlanta, GA 30333
(404) 329-3479

NATIONAL HOTLINE: 1-800-342-2437 (tape); 1-800-447-2437
                              (staffed)
                              In Atlanta: (404) 329-1290 (tape);
                              329-1295 (staffed)

Alcohol, Drug Abuse, and Mental Health Administration
   (ADAMHA)
Parklawn Building
5600 Fishers Lane
Rockville, MD 20857
(301) 443-4797

National Institutes of Health
Building 1
900 Rockville Turnpike
Bethesda, MD 20205

National Cancer Institute
Building 31, National Institutes of Health
900 Rockville Turnpike
Bethesda, MD 20205
(301) 496-5615

National Institute of Allergy and Infectious Diseases
Building 31, National Institutes of Health
900 Rockville Turnpike
Bethesda, MD 20205
(301) 496-2263

National Heart, Lung, and Blood Institute
Building 31, National Institutes of Health
900 Rockville Turnpike
Bethesda, MD 20205
(301) 496-5166

Blood and Blood Products Division
U.S. Food and Drug Administration
Room 220, NIH Building 29
Bethesda, MD 21235
(301) 496-4396

U.S. Social Security Administration
900 Altmeyer Building
Baltimore, MD 21235
(301) 594-3120

Health Care Financing Administration
Hubert H. Humphrey Building
Washington, D.C. 21235
(202) 245-6726

CANADA

Fort Rouge Medical Clinic
601 Coryden Avenue
Winnipeg, R3L 0P3
Manitoba, Ca

GAYS IN HEALTH CARE (GHC)
PO Box 7086 Station A
Toronto, MSW 1x7
Ontario, Ca

AIDS Committee TORONTO (ACT)
PO Box 55 Station F
Toronto M4Y 2L4
Ontario, Ca

AIDS Vancouver
1033 Davie Street, Suite 509
Vancouver, British Columbia

Montreal Health Press
PO Box 1000 Station G
Montreal H2W 2H1
Quebec, Ca

AIDS Network of Edmonton
10233 98th Street
Edmonton, T5J 0M7
Alberta, Ca

MAC AIDS
Metro Area Committee on AIDS
Box 1013, Station M
Halifax B3J 2X1
Nova Scotia, Ca

Canadian Gay Alliance
PO Box 639 Station A
Toronto M5W 1G2
Ontario, Ca

Hassle Free Clinics/AIDS Comm.
556 Church St. #2
Toronto M4Y 2E3
Ontario, Ca

Index